THE SCOTTISH MOUNTAIN GUIDE

BILL ROBERTSON was born and educated in Slamannan in Stirlingshire. He started walking in his late twenties and is now an experienced hill walker. He lives in Edinburgh where he works in the Department of Psychology at Edinburgh University.

THE SCOTTISH MOUNTAIN GUIDE

The Essential Reference Guide
for Hill Walkers and Climbers

Bill Robertson

MAINSTREAM
PUBLISHING

EDINBURGH AND LONDON

I would like to dedicate this guide to my mother, Margaret, for putting up with me for all these years, and also to the memory of my father, Andrew

First published in Great Britain in 1993 by
MAINSTREAM PUBLISHING COMPANY (EDINBURGH) LTD
7 Albany Street
Edinburgh EH1 3UG

ISBN 1 85158 526 5

A catalogue record for this book is available from the British Library

Typeset in Cheltenham by Litho Link Ltd., Welshpool, Powys
Printed in Great Britain by Mackays of Chatham, Chatham

Contents

Acknowledgments

I would like to thank the following individuals and agencies, for their invaluable help and contributions to the production of this guide: Neil and Tina Macleod for the Gaelic translations, Dr Sue Widdicombe for editorial assistance and photography, George Cuthbert for advice and photography, Ian Fraser (School of Scottish Studies) and Dr Ian Campbell (Dept of English Literature) of Edinburgh University, Ian Bonthrone of RAF Lossiemouth, the Scottish Sports Council, the Highland and Islands Enterprise Board and the Scottish Tourist Board.

I would also wish to thank the following people for their general advice, computing knowledge and for lending me their OS maps: Jim Cuthbert, Paul Hutton, Prof Dave Lee, Dr Hamish MacLeod, Dr Tom Pitcairn, Denis Rewt, Arthur Stewart and Roy Welensky.

Introduction

The Highlands and Islands of Scotland have never been more popular. Yet to many of the people who come to explore upland Scotland – both foreign visitors and native Scots – the meanings of the names given to the mountains and hills remain mysterious and obscure. It was my own frustration at not being able to find a useable guide that led me to write this book.

It is my intention that this book should be both a source of reference and a practical guide. However, it has been designed as a reference work to be taken to the hills rather than left at home. To make best use of this guide, it should be used in conjunction with Ordnance Survey maps, especially the maps of the Landranger 1 : 50,000 series.

In the sections on mountains access and safety I make no apology for presenting an account which takes the most basic rules of mountain safety as its starting point. This book is aimed at people exploring the Scottish mountains for the first time, as well as seasoned hill walkers – and even old hands sometimes need a gentle reminder. In these sections I have tried to explain the rationale behind good mountain practice, rather than providing a simple list of dos and don'ts.

The broad aim of this book is to introduce Gaelic to a wider audience. If it helps to stir your interest in the language and increase your enjoyment of the mountains then it will have gone some way towards achieving this aim.

1. HOW TO USE
THE SCOTTISH MOUNTAIN GUIDE

Using the translation section

The main section of this guide is a reference section providing Gaelic-English translations for the mountains of upland Scotland. To make best use of this section, it should be used in conjunction with maps of the Ordnance Survey Landranger 1:50 000 series. The following steps explain how to obtain a translation for a chosen feature:

1. Locate the feature on the map and read off its elevation. (This is the key piece of information needed to locate a translation.)

2. Turn to the appropriate page in the translation section. (The pages in this section are referred to using the Landranger map names and numbers listed on page 14 and shown on the outline map on page 13 The same names and numbers can be found on the purple covers attached to Ordnance Survey maps.)

3. Use the elevation to find the feature you are interested in and read off the pronunciation and translation. All hills are arranged in descending order of height.

The information provided for a feature is laid out as follows:

❏ Munro / ◯ Corbett Indicator
Height in metres
                Name on map   Translation   Map reference
 | | | |

❏ **1245m** **Cairn Gorm** .... Blue Mountain 005041
    4085ft karn gor-om [kayr-n gor-m]
    | |

Height in feet   Pronunciation

Notes

1. *Munro and Corbett Indicators*

   These symbols are used to denote hills which appear in the Munro and Corbett tables and designed to allow you to keep a record of the hills you have climbed by shading in the symbol.

2. *Elevations*

   The tables provide information for all peaks over 610m (2000ft) on the mainland (a lesser height is used for the islands). Elevations on Landranger maps are expressed in metres in the form of contours and spot heights. However, this section provides height in both metres and feet, as the Munro and Corbett tables still list elevations in feet.

3. *Mountain Names*

   Where a mountain has several peaks, the mountain name appears without a height against it. However, an elevation is provided for the peak which forms the highest part of the mountain. For example:

	An Teallach......................	The Forge	
	an t-yeel-ach		
	Highest peak :		
❏ **1062m**	**Bidein à Ghlas Thuill**.......	Peak of the Green.............	069843
3484ft	beet-yan a chlas tool	Hollow	

4. *Translations*

   All translations have been made by the author, and any discrepancies are his sole responsibility.

5. *Map References*

   Six-figure map references are provided for mountains which appear in the Munro and Corbett tables. (An explanation of six-figure references can be found inside the cover of all OS maps.)

6. *Pronunciation*

   All phonetic pronunciations are as you would find in the Gaelic dictionary. Pronunciations in brackets indicate more common, modern pronunciations.

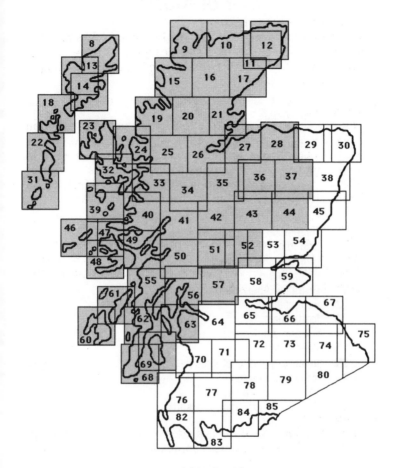

© Crown Copyright

Area Covered by the Guide

List of Maps

To keep an inventory of your maps, mark the appropriate box.

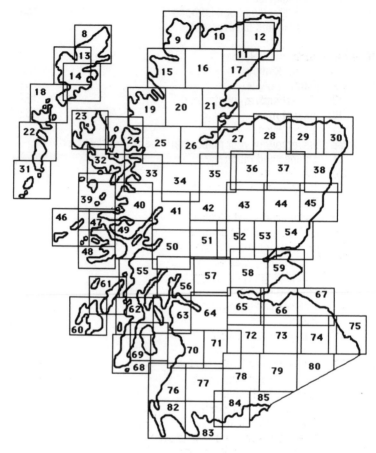

Inventory Map

(Keep an inventory of your maps by shading the appropriate grid)

Other Scottish Landranger Maps

Map No.	Name
☐ 29	Banff
☐ 30	Fraserburgh and Peterhead
☐ 38	Aberdeen
☐ 45	Stonehaven
☐ 53	Blairgowrie
☐ 54	Dundee and Montrose
☐ 58	Perth to Alloa
☐ 59	St.Andrews and Kirkcaldy
☐ 64	Glasgow
☐ 65	Falkirk and West Lothian
☐ 66	Edinburgh and Midlothian
☐ 67	Duns, Dunbar and Eyemouth
☐ 70	Ayr and Kilmarnock
☐ 71	Lanark and Upper Nithsdale
☐ 72	Upper Clyde Valley
☐ 73	Peebles and Galashiels
☐ 74	Kelso
☐ 75	Berwick-Upon-Tweed
☐ 76	Girvan
☐ 77	Dalmellington to New Galloway
☐ 78	Nithsdale and Annandale
☐ 79	Hawick and Eskdale
☐ 80	Cheviot Hills and Kielder
☐ 82	Stanraer and Glenluce
☐ 83	Newton Stewart and Kirkcudbright
☐ 84	Dumfries and Castle Douglas
☐ 85	Carlisle and Solway Firth

Corbetts not Covered by maps in this guide

Map 71 Lanark and Upper Nithsdale
○ **800m** (2756ft)   Broad Law   146235

Map 77 Dalmellington to New Galloway
○ **843m** (2766ft)   Merrick   428855
○ **797m** (2715ft)   Cairnsmore of Carsphairn   594980
○ **768m** (2520ft)   Shalloch on Minnoch   405907

Map 78 Nithsdale and Annandale
○ **808m** (2651ft)   Hart Fell   113135

Map 79 Hawick and Eskdale
○ **822m** (2697ft)   White Coomb   163151

2. MOUNTAIN NAMES AND TERMS

Mountain Names

Why are the mountains and peaks of Scotland named as they are?

Most of the names are quite straightforward since they are derived from descriptions of the mountains and peaks. For example, some names describe their appearance: rocky, rough, mossy, heathered, and so on. Others are named after a colour, possibly at a particular time of the year when the mountains took on a distinctive hue: red, green, blue or white for example. Names may also have been given according to shape, e.g. round, jagged or long.

Another way of naming the mountains seems to have been based on associations with tree species (such as pine, rowan and yew). Similarly, some names incorporate the names of animals and birds (deer, goat, pig, eagle and dove for instance) which may have been abundant at the time of naming. However the origins of other names are less obvious: we can only guess at the reasons why some names include terms such as butter, lonely, trembling and milkmaid.

Some mountains had their names changed (possibly by the local inhabitants) introducing a corrupt form of the language, for example gowal (gobhal), chonzie (choanneach), lawers (labhar), lui (loagh), nevis (neibheis), starav (starbh), vane (mheadhon), vorlich (mhurlaig). (See Mountain Components List on page 166 for translation of words in brackets.)

Other names have been translated into English from their original Gaelic name, probably by English-speaking landlords moving into the area or even by the local inhabitants themselves. Others still retain the Norse name, such as Ainshval, Askival, Resipol, given to them by our Nordic invaders. These hills are mainly situated in the far north-west and the Western Isles.

Finally, languages like Gaelic inevitably change over the centuries (Olde English to modern English for example).

When documents, such as maps, are passed from one generation to the next, the words may retain the same form and spelling as the original. Books, on the other hand, are edited and in the process, changes in the language pass into the new generation of text. Thus some of the words used on today's maps do not correspond to the modern Gaelic spelling, and many of them have become so obscure or corrupt that a translation has been impossible to find.

The Origins of the Gaelic Language

The Gaelic language owes its origins to the ancient Celtic (Goidelic) language. This language was used by the tribes inhabiting Western Europe at the time the Romans dominated the area 2000 years ago. It was introduced to Scotland from Ireland c.AD 500 by settlers and missionaries moving into south-west Scotland, especially Argyll. These settlers (and their language) spread outward over the next several centuries and their language gradually replaced that spoken by the inhabitants of northern Scotland.

During the centuries that followed, Norse settlers started invading these shores. They landed mainly in the northern isles, the north-west coast and the Western Isles. As their settlements became a permanent feature of the landscape, Norse words were incorporated into the Celtic language. Spoken Norse, however, started to die out after the loss of the Norse colonies in Scotland after the Battle of Largs (1263).

The Gaelic language started to decline before this, however, partly due to King Malcolm Canmore's (1031-93) marriage to Queen Margaret who was an English-only speaker. Together they banned the Gaelic language from the Royal Court and replaced it with English. Over the next several centuries, only English was spoken by Lowland Scots and Scots living in the more fertile lands of the east coast. Eventually only the inhabitants of west central Scotland the north-west and the Western Isles spoke the Gaelic tongue.

The Gaelic language declined even further during the periods known as the Highland Clearances (1780-1820 and 1840-1854). The landlords of the western areas began ousting the inhabitants living and crofting the land in order to use it for sheep farming. The inhabitants who had been forcibly removed from their crofts and homes were dispersed to all corners of the western world. As a consequence, the Gaelic language is spoken as a 'first language' only by the inhabitants of the Western Isles and small pockets of people living on the north-west coast.

Therefore, although it has borrowed from other languages, the Gaelic language, as it is used today, derives directly from the Irish language, as Irish and Scottish languages were similar until c.AD 1000. At the present time, Gaelic is spoken by less than 90,000 people in a population of over five million. The majority of these speakers, using it as a 'second language', now live in the Glasgow area where they have had to settle in recent years due to a shortage of work opportunities in the area in which they were born. A revival is under way, however, with various Gaelic societies and television shows promoting the Gaelic language. Many Scots are now taking this opportunity to learn their 'mother tongue' as a second language.

Mountain Words in Gaelic

The following words are all used to describe high ground in Scotland: *aonach*, *ben*, *beinn*, *cairn*, *carn*, *mam*, *meall*, *monadh*, *mounth*, and *tom*. They can all be found in the Gaelic dictionary, where they are defined as a mountain, a hill or a large mound shape. This poses a question: at what height does a hill become a mountain in Scotland?

Meall a'Bhuiridh for example is 1108m (3635ft) high and in the same area Beinn na Gucaig at 616m (2020ft) is little more than half its height. Since dictionaries state that the word *meall* means hill and *beinn* [ben] means mountain, it suggests an equivalence between the two features and yet there is clearly a great difference in height. Therefore in this guide I have decided to use the word mountain, as a translation for the above words when they are associated with Munros, over 914m (3000ft). For high ground below this height, I have used the translation 'hill'.

Gaelic Pronunciation Guide

The Gaelic language is complex, because of its origins. It is also difficult to phonetisise because many of its sounds are made in the throat. This also makes it difficult to reproduce as a written syllable. Moreover, its pronunciation varies from island to island and area to area, and, like other languages it has regional dialects. Such variations increase the difficulties of giving a clear written description of the spoken word. (The Gaelic alphabet contains only 18 letters: it does not have J, K, Q, V, W, X, Y or Z.) Hopefully the guide laid out below will go some way towards alleviating this difficulty and help with the pronunciation of the Gaelic words used to describe high ground in Scotland.

All translated words used in this guide are based upon English words or syllables, rather than the cumbersome phonetic key tables that are found in dictionaries.

Vowels

a	p**a**t
e	b**e**d
i	h**i**t
o	l**ow**
u	**u**tter

Consonants

b	**b**at
c	**c**ar
d	**d**art
f	**f**ar
g	**g**one
j	**j**ust
k	**k**ey
l	**l**aw
m	**m**an
n	**n**ut
r	**r**ain
s	**s**in
t	**t**ap
v	**v**at
y	**y**ou

Syllables

ah	denoting surprise
ay	b**ay**
arv	st**arve**
aw	l**aw**
ch	Ba**ch** (composer)
ee	s**ee**d
oa	b**oa**t
oo	s**oo**t
om	h**om**e
our	s**our**
osh	g**osh**
ou	s**ou**p
orry	s**orry**
ow	h**ow**
oy	b**oy**
yle	st**yle**

The letter *h* following the first letter of a word (e.g. *ah*, *bh*, *ch*), only changes the pronunciation of the word, not the meaning. Loch, meaning a Scottish lake, is often mis-pronounced by visitors to this country. The proper pronunciation of the word *loch* is *law-ch*. (See guide.)

Munros and Corbetts

The term Munro comes from the name of the late Sir Hugh Thomas Munro, an original member of the Scottish Mountaineering Club which was founded in the late 19th century. He was an enthusiastic hill walker who had a keen interest in the mountains of Scotland, especially those over 3000ft (914.4m). This in turn prompted him to try and climb all hills over this height, and to compile his own list of all known mountains at or above this height. When his original list was first published in 1891 the term Munro was coined by his fellow enthusiasts and used thereafter to describe a mountain over 3000ft in the Scottish Highlands. In the decades that followed his death, his original list was amended several times with the development of more accurate measuring apparatus. The list is now controlled by the Scottish Mountaineering Club (S.M.C.) and known as Munro's Tables. It contains a list of 277 separate mountains and 240 peaks (commonly known as tops) over 3000ft. There is, however, some controversy amongst some people in the hill-walking fraternity over what constitutes a Munro in today's terms and therefore over the total number of Munros in Scotland. Some would like to return to Sir Hugh Munro's original list, which contained 283 mountains and 255 tops; others argue for retaining the revised version. At present this contoversy is unresolved. I do not wish to enter into this disagreement, although some of today's hill walkers, commonly known as Munroists or Munro baggers, have made it their life's ambition to climb all the Munros listed in the tables, and climb only these. But as you will see in your travels throughout the Highlands, there are many beautiful hills of a lesser height, which are just as interesting to climb and admire as a Munro.

Corbett is the term used to describe a hill which is between 762m (2,500ft) and 914.4m (3,000ft) in height with a clear ascent of 152m (500ft) on every side which separates it from any adjacent hill. The word Corbett also originates from a person's name: Mr John Rooke Corbett was a member of the

S.M.C. until the late 1930s and, like Sir Hugh Munro, a keen hill walker. He decided to set about climbing and making a list of all the Scottish hills between these heights with the aim of having his list published. The Corbett Tables, like the Munro Tables, have been amended over the years, and with deletions and inclusions, today's list stands at 221. This list is also administered by the Scottish Mountaineering Club (S.M.C.).

3. MOUNTAIN SAFETY AND PRACTICE

Mountain Access

Access to the Scottish Highlands has changed over the years. There was a time when people could roam at will, normally with the consent of the local landowner. If the walker observed the country code and showed respect for the landowner's property, he or she was allowed the freedom of the mountains.

Today's landowners, however, run their estates as businesses and they rely on the money they receive during the hunting and shooting season for the upkeep of their land. Therefore hill walkers are not welcome on their land during the following seasons:

Grouse: 12 August to 10 December.
Deer stalking (Stags): 1 September to 20 October.
Deer culling (Hinds): 20 October to 15 February.

The lambing season which runs from March to May should also be observed by hill walkers, and at no time during this period should dog owners allow their pets to run free on the hillsides. If you happen to 'trespass' on to their land during the shooting season or at any other time, the landowners have the right to ask you to leave the area. If you refuse they are within their legal rights to use 'reasonable force' to eject you from their land. Trespass is not a criminal offence in Scotland, but if you are a persistent offender, the landowner can obtain a court order to prevent you from ever entering the land again. Moreover, if during 'trespass' individuals are seen causing wilful damage (broken fences, gates etc), the landowner can sue them for damages to cover the cost of repair or replacement.

There is however, land that is not affected by the hunting season and access to these areas is available all year round. This land is owned by the National Trust for Scotland

and the Nature Conservancy Council. These areas are clearly marked on Ordnance Survey maps. There will, of course, be times when small areas are sectioned off to allow 'land maintenance' to be carried out, and you will be asked to by-pass these areas to give the land time to recover.

If you are in any doubt about access to an area you wish to walk in, consult the local landowner, stalker or gamekeeper, if known, or ask locally for advice. The local constabulary are usually very helpful on questions regarding access to the local estates. If shooting is taking place in an area where you wish to walk, an alternative route may be suggested to you.

Hill walkers should also be reminded that access to most estates is along private roads which should not be driven on without prior permission. In addition, parking your car on these roads, blocking gateways or any other land for that matter should be avoided at all times as this can cause accidents to other road users.

Abide by these simple instructions and you cannot go wrong.

COUNTRY CODE

- Enjoy the countryside and respect its life and work.
- Guard against all risks of fire.
- Fasten all gates.
- Keep dogs under close control.
- Keep to paths across farm land.
- Use gates and stiles to cross fences, hedges, and walls.
- Leave livestock, crops and machinery alone.
- Help to keep all water clean.
- Protect wildlife, wild plants and trees.
- Go carefully on country roads.
- Make no unnecessary noise.
- Take your litter home.

Mountain Safety

1. Before setting out on any trip, obtain a weather forecast by phoning the relevant number.
   (See Weather Call Map.)

2. Always plan your route carefully and consider the nature of the ground and distance to be covered. (See Walking Speed Table.)

3. Always leave a note with a responsible person, giving details of your planned route and any bad weather alternatives, the number of people in your party and the time you expect to return. Report your safe return.

4. Always set out with the proper equipment. (See Equipment Checklist.)

MAIN DANGERS

Tracks and Paths
Part of Scotland's attraction lies in the wildness of its countryside. Few paths are sign-posted and even those clearly marked on maps may be difficult to trace. It's very easy to follow a sheep or deer track that leads to nowhere. Use your compass and check your location at all times.

Shelter and Stopping Points
Carry extra warm clothing and food supplies, since you may not find a sheltered stopping point on your walk. Mountain shelters (bothies) are marked on maps but are not easy to locate.

Snow
During the summer months you may find patches of winter snow. You should avoid these areas unless you have the skills to cope with the extra hazards. The snow will be hard, icy and very slippery. Remember – serious accidents can result from a 'simple slip'.

Children
As a general rule, take children only on routes which allow a safe and easy retreat. Do not take young children on long walks.

Accidents

If one of your party has an accident and cannot be moved:
1. Mark your exact position on the map.
2. Treat any injuries as best you can.
3. If possible, leave someone to care for the casualty while others descend with the map to get help.
4. Telephone rescue services (by dialling 999) and ask for the police.
5. Report the map grid reference where you left the casualty and details of the casualty's condition.

Casualties

Casualties may have to stay on the hills for a long time or even overnight. They should be made comfortable and left with a survival bag, lots of warm clothing, spare food and drink, something eye-catching to attract attention, and a torch and whistle. Hypothermia and shock are the main dangers in this situation.

Emergency Signals
Six blasts on the whistle or *six flashes with the torch*

(Reproduced with the kind permission of the Scottish Mountain Safety Group of the Scottish Sports Council.)

WINTER SNOWS (AVALANCHES)

The risk of avalanche on the mountains of Scotland is real. Accordingly the Scottish Avalanche Information Service and the Glasgow Weather Centre provide information on avalanche conditions for the following areas: Glencoe, Cairngorm, Lochaber and Lochnagar. This information is for areas outwith the ski resorts and is broadcast on radio and TV, published in weather reports and displayed on notice-boards in the aforementioned areas. It includes a risk factor on the five-point scale below:

Category 1
(Very Low) Usually applies in conditions where névé (very hard snow) exists, with no new snowfall or drifting. Slow thaw of old snow could also produce this nearly zero-risk situation.

Category 2
(Low) Generally stable snowpack, with minimum risk of large avalanches. Any new snow is stable; old snow, either hard frozen or thawing, is unlikely to produce wet slides.

Category 3
(Medium)   Accumulations of new snow or slab (crusty layer) are unlikely to be deeper than 30 cm (12ins) and are generally stable, although localised avalanches are possible. In thaw conditions, wet sluffs (soft, deep, wet snow) are possible, but large slabs are unlikely. Occasional spontaneous avalanching is possible.

Category 4
(High)   High risk of victim-triggered avalanche of any type, with the possibility of large avalanches, some spontaneous avalanching possible.

Category 5
(Very High) Extreme risk of spontaneous avalanche of any kind, including the the largest wet or dry slabs (crusty layers).

Note: Cornices
Cornice (snow overhang) collapse is a specialised type of avalanche, often independent of general risk. When cornice danger is known to exist, it will be specified.

(Reproduced with the kind permission of Scottish Sports Council.)

WARNING
Do not assume that avalanches only occur in the areas covered by the S.A.I.S. These are high-risk areas because they are popular with the public at times when snow is deep on the ground. Avalanches do occur in other areas and can be just as dangerous for individuals. Therefore, ask locally about avalanche possibilities in the area you wish to cover and if in doubt, modify your plans accordingly.

SEARCH AND RESCUE HELICOPTERS

The area covered in this guide is covered by search and rescue helicopters from three bases in Scotland: RAF Lossiemouth in the north and HMS Gannet in the south, both with Sea Kings, and RAF Leuchars in the east with Wessex helicopters. (At the time of writing some doubts exist over the future of the base at Leuchars.) The two Sea King bases provide 24-hours-a-day 365-days-a-year cover and although their primary role is to rescue downed aircrew, they are frequently used in mountain rescue operations and have been instrumental in saving many lives. Helicopters must only be seen as complementary to the rescue teams as they cannot fly in fog, dense mist, cloud or blizzards, but may be used for transporting the rescue team nearer to an incident and for speedy evacuation of a casualty to a hospital. In fair weather conditions or at night the helicopter may well be first on the scene of an incident and the following information will help both the casualty and the helicopter crew:

On reporting an incident.
1. Relate a position to natural feature e.g. corrie floor, ridge or loch, as well as giving an accurate grid reference. (A 100-metre error in a map reference could mean hours of searching on a ridge line.)

2. If the casualty is injured do not forget to report these injuries to the police as it will help in prioritising the rescue: you may not be the only people in difficulty that day.

3. Describe the equipment and clothing worn by the casualty and anyone attending them as well as possible. The most important detail is colour.

Casualties.
1. Once you have sent for help **do not move**; apart from exposing yourself to more danger you will only hinder the efforts of the helicopter and rescue parties.

2. Wear clothing that will stand out against your surroundings.

When the helicopter arrives.
1. **Do not** try to get to the helicopter; let it come to you.
2. **Do** indicate you need assistance.
3. **Do** follow the instructions of the helicopter winchman and explain your situation to him.

It is important that the above information is followed in order to provide every assistance to the helicopter and yourselves. Once on the scene the helicopter winchman will administer any medical aid needed and decide upon the best form of evacuation. With large parties this may involve leaving some people on the ground for later evacuation. With small parties or parties in dangerous positions, it may be more sensible to evacuate everyone together.
(Written by Mr Ian Bonthrone AEMT, Helicopter Search and Rescue, RAF Lossiemouth.)

These symbols are the international rescue signs recognised by search and rescue teams.

We want help:

We do not want anything

red flare or   square of red
light   cloth laid out

Mountain Equipment

Clothing
Warm, wind and waterproof clothing is essential. This should include gloves, a hat, fully waterproof and windproof jacket and trousers, and spare clothing such as a warm sweater. These should always be carried as a precaution against changes in the weather, which can occur with alarming speed: even on warm, sunny days, bad weather might be on the way. So, if the wind strengthens, cloud thickens, visibility decreases or the temperature falls, turn back or find shelter. In poor visibility always use your map and compass. Never set out without protective clothing. Walkers who take to the hills dressed in T-shirt and jeans endanger not only themselves but also those who may have to assist them to reach shelter.

Footwear
Your footwear should provide good ankle support and have a firm sole with a secure grip. Hill-walking boots are strongly recommended. Sport shoes are not recommended as they give no ankle support and no protection from falling stones that may be dislodged when crossing rocky areas.

Equipment
Always carry a map and compass and know how to use them. Ordnance Survey maps scale 1:50,000 or 1:25,000 are recommended. Carry equipment for use in an emergency, such as a torch, whistle, first aid kit and survival bag. These items are inexpensive and readily available from all outdoor sports shops. In your first aid kit take some plasters, dressings and

bandages. Your survival bag is also very useful for sitting on where the ground is damp and muddy, when you have to take a rest or a food stop.

Food and Drink
Take ample food and drink for each member of your group. You will not be able to buy any on the hills. Always take reserve supplies. Simple, high-energy foods, e.g. chocolate, dried fruits, cheese and biscuits are best, as are hot drinks in cold, wet weather. All the above items can be carried in a day sack, which is also very useful for taking your litter home.

Equipment Checklist

All Year Round

waterproofs	torch
gloves	whistle
hat	First Aid kit
warm sweater	survival Bag
boots	food
socks	flask
maps	day sack
compass	

Winter Snow Walking

extra warm clothes	gaiters
crampons	ropes
ice axe	snow shovel
over gloves	extra food
snow goggles	

Enjoy your walk
Find out about local walks by contacting your nearest Tourist Information Centre.

Country Code
Know and follow the country code (see page 26) and respect the activities of other users of the countryside.

Winter Walking
Walking in winter requires extra precautions. Daylight hours are shorter and bad weather is more severe. Knowledge of winter walking should be gained from experienced hill-walkers. Inexperienced walkers should not attempt long walks or climbs in winter.

4. MOUNTAIN GUIDE

8 Stornoway and North Lewis
13 West Lewis and North Harris

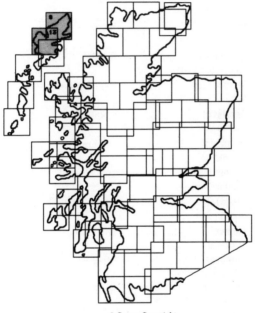

© Crown Copyright

8 STORNOWAY AND NORTH LEWIS

No significant high ground in this area

13 WEST LEWIS AND NORTH HARRIS

Height	Mountain	Translation
743m	**Mulla fo-Dheas**................	South Ridge
2437ft	mool-la fo jess	
729m	**Uisgnaval Mor**	Big Outer Hill
2391ft	u-is-gna-val more	

Height	Mountain	Translation
697m 2286ft	**Teilesval** teel-es-val	unknown
679m 2227ft	**Tirga Mor** tir-ka more	unknown
662m 2171ft	**Oreval** or-e-val	Moor Fowl Hill
659m 2162ft	**Ullaval** ool-la-val	Wolf Hill
614m 2014ft	**Mullach an Langa** mool-lach an lan-ka	Long Ridge
579m 1899ft	**Stulaval** stool-a-val	Enclosure Hill
574m 1883ft	**Mealisval** meel-is-val	Stony Farm
572m 1876ft	**Beinn Mhor** bay-n [ben] voar	Big Hill
559m 1834ft	**Sgaoth Aird** skou ard	High Steep Hill
556m 1824ft	**Ceartaval** k-er-ta-val	unknown
552m 1811ft	**Tomnaval** tom-na-val	unknown
531m 1742m	**Sgaoth Iosal** skou ees-al	Low Steep Hill
523m 1715ft	**Uisgaval** u-is-gna-val	Small Outer Hill
515m 1689ft	**Tahaval** ta-ha-val	unknown
514m 1686ft	**Cracaval** kra-ka-val	Crow Hill
511m 1676ft	**Cleiseval** klees-e-val	Rocky Hill
505m 1656ft	**Laival a'Tuath** lay-val a too-ah	Low Hill of the North
501m 1643ft	**Laival a'Deas** lay-val a jess	Low Hill of the South
497m 1630ft	**Griomaval** grim-a-val	Grim's Hill
497m 1630ft	**Teinnasval** teen-as-val	unknown
492m 1614ft	**Liuthaid** loo-tat	Numerous
491m 1611ft	**Sron Scourst** srawn skoorst	Point of the Valley Crossing a Ridge
489m 1604ft	**Husival** hoos-i-val	Horse-shaped Hill

Height	Mountain	Translation
486m	**Carn Ban**	White Hill
1594ft	karn ban	
473m	**Mullach a'Ruisg**	Bare Summit
1548ft	mool-ach a rooshk	
470m	**Gormol**	Blue Hill
1542ft	gor-mol	
467m	**Tamanaisval**	Harbour Hill
1532ft	tam-an-is-val	
454m	**Muladal**	Promontory Valley
1489ft	mool-a-dal	
453m	**Oreval**	Moor Fowl Hill
1486ft	or-e-val	
452m	**Naidevala**	unknown
1483ft	nay-da-vala	
449m	**Caiteshal**..........................	The Castle
1473ft	kate-shal	
447m	**Crionaig**	Little Hill
1466ft	kreen-ak	
442m	**Sron Ulladale**...................	Wolf Point
1450ft	srawn ull-a-dale	
429m	**Suainaval**.........................	Sweyn's Hill
1407ft	soon-a-val	
425m	**Sgianait**	The Knives
1394ft	skee-an-at	
424m	**Muaithabal**	Narrow Hill
1391ft	moo-ta-bal	
412m	**Leosaval**	Ljot's Hill
1351ft	los-a-val	
411m	**Tarain**	unknown
1348ft	tar-in	
401m	**Mor Monadh**	Big Moor
1315ft	more mon-ah	
397m	**Beinn Meadhonach**..........	Middle Hill
1302ft	bay-n [ben] vee-yon-ach	
389m	**Straiaval**	unknown
1276ft	stray-a-val	
389m	**An Coileach**	The Cockerel
1276ft	an kil-yach	
389m	**Beinn na h-Uamha**...........	Hill of the Caves
1276ft	bay-n [ben] na hoo-va	
379m	**Beinn a'Mhuill**.................	Hill of the Mill
1243ft	bay-n [ben] a vool	
378m	**Kearnaval**	unknown
1240ft	keer-na-val	
376m	**Tarsaval**...........................	unknown
1233ft	tars-a-val	

Height	Mountain	Translation
376m 1233ft	**Mo Vigadale** .... mo vig-a-dale	Vigleif's Valley
376m 1233ft	**Kearnaval** .... keer-na-val	unknown
371m 1217ft	**Uisenis** .... u-is-en-is	Isthmus Point
370m 1214ft	**Beinn a'Mhuill** .... bay-n [ben] a vool	Hill of the Mound
354m 1161ft	**Mula Chalartan** .... mool-a chal-ar-tan	unknown
351m 1151ft	**Beinn a'Deas** .... bay-n [ben] a jess	South Hill
336m 1102ft	**Cipeagil Bheal** .... keep-a-gil vi-al	Bowl-shaped Ravine
334m 1096ft	**Uiseval** .... u-is-e-val	Isthmus Hill
328m 1076ft	**Clett Ard** .... klett ard	High Ridge
327m 1072ft	**Feirhisval** .... feer-his-val	unknown
308m 1010ft	**Beinn a'Both** .... bay-n [ben] bow	Hill of the Hut
306m 1003ft	**Husival Beag** .... hoos-i-val bay-k [beg]	Little Horse-shaped Hill

9 Cape Wrath
(1 Munro)
(6 Corbetts)

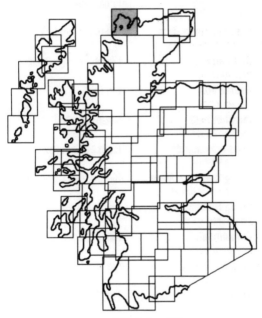

© Crown Copyright

9 CAPE WRATH

Height	Mountain	Translation	Map Ref.
❑ **927m** 3041ft	**Ben Hope** ben hope	Mountain of the Bay	477501
○ **911m** 2989ft	**Foinaven** foy-nay-ven	Hill of White Water	317507
901m 2956ft	**Ceann Garbh** k-yann garv	Rough Head	
○ **801m** 2628ft	**Meallan Liath Coire Mhic Dhughaill** me-yal-an lee-ah cora [korry] vic doo-al	Grey Hill of MacDougall's Hollow	357392
○ **800m** 2624ft	**Cranstackie** kran-staky	Rugged Peak	351556
○ **787m** 2581ft	**Arkle** ar-kil	Hill of the Level Top	303462
○ **777m** 2550ft	**Meall Horn** me-yal horn	Hill of the Cairn	353449

Height	Mountain	Translation	Map Ref.
○ 772m 2532ft	**Beinn Spionnaidh** .... bay-n [ben] spee-on-nay	Hill of Strength	362573
752m 2467ft	**Meall Garbh** .... me-yal garv	Rough Hill	
729m 2391ft	**Sabhal Beag** .... sav-al bay-k [beg]	Little Barn	
729m 2391ft	**Creagan Meall Horn** .... kray-kan me-yal horn	Hill of the Rocky Cairn	
721m 2369ft	**Ben Stack** .... ben stack	Hill of the High Peak	
703m 2306ft	**Sabhal Mor** .... sav-al more	Big Barn	
601m 1971ft	**Meallan Liath** .... me-yal-an lee-ah	Small Grey Hill	
589m 1932ft	**Cnoc a'Mhadaidh**............ krok a va-tay	Hillock of the Fox	
514m 1686ft	**Creag Riabhach Mhor**...... kray-k ree-vach voar	Big Grizzled Rock	
485m 1591ft	**Creag Riabhach** .... kray-k ree-vach	Grizzled Rock	
482m 1581ft	**Conamheall** .... kon-a-ve-yal	Hill of the Meeting	
468m 1535ft	**Lurg an Tabhail** .... loork an ta-vil	Stem of Understanding	
467m 1532ft	**An Grianan** .... an gree-nan	The Sunny Spot	
464m 1522ft	**Meall na Moine** .... me-yal na moy-na	Hill of the Peat	
457m 1499ft	**Fashven** .... fash-ven	Rising Hill	
454m 1489ft	**Creag Staonsaid** .... kray-k stoun-sat	Curved Rocks	
423m 1387ft	**Beinn Dearg**.................... bay-n [ben] jer-ak	Red Hill	
403m 1322ft	**Creag Riabhach Bheag**.... kray-k ree-vach vay-k [beg]	Small Grizzled Rock	
392m 1286ft	**Creag Riabhach** .... kray-k ree-vach	Grizzled Rock	
371m 1217ft	**Sgribhis Bheinn** .... skree-vish vay-n [ven]	Rocky Hillside	
348ft 1141ft	**Cnoc a'Craois** .... krok a kroush	Hillock of the Cross	
332m 1089ft	**Ghlas Bheinn** .... chlas vay-n [ven]	Green Hill	
316m 1036ft	**Meall na Moine** .... me-yal na moy-na	Hill of the Peat	

10 Strathnaver
(1 Corbett)

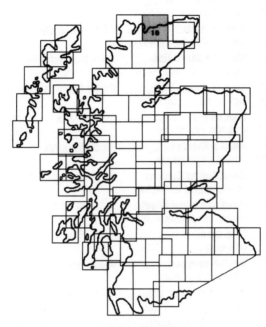

© Crown Copyright

10 STRATHNAVER

Height	Mountain	Translation	Map Ref.
	Ben Loyal ben loy-al Highest peak:	Elm Tree Hill	
○ **764m** 2506ft	**An Caisteal** an kash-tyal	The Castle	578489
714m 2342ft	**Carn an Tional** karn an tee-on-al	Hill of the Collecting	
708m 2296ft	**Sgor Chaonasaid** skoor chou-na-shat	Peak of the Weeping	
642m 2106ft	**Sgor a'Chleirich** skor a chler-eech	Peak of the Clergyman	
592m 1942ft	**Ben Grian Mor** ben gree-an more	Big Dark Hill	
580m 1902ft	**Ben Grian Beg** ben gree-an beg	Small Dark Hill	
557m 1829ft	**Cnoc na Cuilean** krok na kool-an	Hillock of the Pup	

Height	Mountain	Translation
441m 1446ft	**Creag Dubh**...................... kray-k doo	Black Rock
432m 1417ft	**Carn a'Mhadaidh**............. karn a va-tay	Hill of the Fox
388m 1273ft	**Meall a'Bhreac-Leathad**.. me-yal a brechk [breck] lay-hat	Hill of the Speckled Slope
368m 1207ft	**Meall an Spothaidh**......... me-yal an spaw-ta	Hill of the Castrating
356m 1168ft	**Cnoc an Daimh Mor**......... krok an dav more	Big Hillock of the Deer
345m 1131ft	**Cnoc nan Tri-chlach**........ krok nan tree chlach	Hillock of the Three Stones
337m 1105ft	**Meall a Bhealaich**........... me-yal a vee-yal-ach	Hill of the Gorge
337m 1105ft	**Meall Bad na Cuaiche**..... me-yal bad na koo-acha	Hill of the Curly Tuft
335m 1099ft	**Meall nan Clach Ruadha**. me-yal nan klach roo-ah	Hill of the Red Rocks
319m 1046ft	**Cnoc Craggie** .... krok krag-gi	Rocky Hillside
318m 1036ft	**Meall Meadhonach**.......... me-yal mee-yon-ach	Middle Hill
310m 1017ft	**Meall Leathad na Craoibh** me-yal lay-hat na krouv	Hill of the Tree Slope
307m 1007ft	**Cnoc an Fhreiceadain**...... krok an free-ka-din	Hillock of the Watcher

11 Thurso and Dunbeath
12 Thurso and Wick
17 Helmsdale and Strath of Kildonan
21 Dornoch, Alness and Invergordon

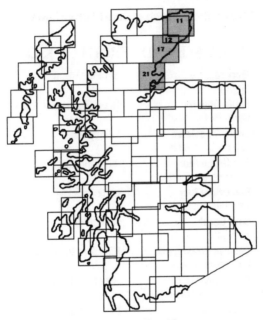

© Crown Copyright

11 THURSO AND DUNBEATH

Height	Mountain	Translation
484m 1588ft	**Maiden Pap** .... may-den pap	Maiden's Breast
348m 1141ft	**Beinn Glas Choire**............. bay-n glas chora [ben glas korry]	Hill of the Grey Hollow
290m 951ft	**Beinn nan Bad Mor**.......... bay-n [bne] nan bad more	Hill of the Big Tuft
283m 928ft	**Cnoc na Feadaige**............. krok na fed-ag	Hillock of the Plover
269m 882ft	**Cnoc an Conachreag**........ krok an cona-chray-k	Hillock of the Mossy Rocks
251m 823ft	**Beinn Ratha** .... bay-n [ben] rah	Fortress Hill

Height	Mountain	Translation
243m 797ft	**Cnoc an Fhuarain Bhain** .. krok an foor-an van	Hillock of the Pale Spring
226m 741ft	**Coire na Beinne** .... cora [korry] na bay-na	Hillock of the Hollow

12 THURSO AND WICK

No significant high ground outwith Map 11

17 HELMSDALE AND STRATH OF KILDONAN

706m 2316ft	**Morven**........................... more-ven	Big Hill
628m 2060ft	**Beinn Dhorain**.................. bay-n [ben] dor-an	Hill of Torment
592m 1942ft	**Beinn Mhealaich** .... bay-n vee-yal-ach	Lumpy Hill
590m 1935ft	**Ben Griam Mor** .... ben gree-am more	Big Dark Hill
580m 1903ft	**Ben Griam Beg** .... ben gree-am beg	Little Dark Hill
545m 1788ft	**Carn Garbh**....................... karn garv	Rough Hill
517m 1696ft	**Cnoc an Eireannaich**........ krok an er-an-ach	Hillock of the Irishman
486m 1594ft	**Beinn Smeorail**................ bay-n [ben] sme-or-al	Hill of the Thrush
484m 1586ft	**Maiden Pap** .... may-den pap	Maiden's Breast
446m 1463ft	**Beinn Lunndaidh** .... bay-n [ben] loon-day	Hill of the Wet Place
422m 1384ft	**Braigh na h-Eaglaishe** ..... bray na heg-lish	Slope of the Church
414m 1358ft	**Beinn Dubhainn** .... bay-n [ben] doo-an	Claw-shaped Hill
405m 1328ft	**Meall a'Bhuirich**.............. me-yal a voor-eech	Hill of the Bellowing
405m 1328ft	**Creag Thoraraidh**............. kray-k tor-ray	Burial Rocks
402m 1319ft	**Cnoc na Maole**................. krok na moula	Bare Hillock
387m 1269ft	**Creag nan Fiadh** .... kra-y nan fee	Rock of the Deer
365m 1197ft	**Cnoc na Breun Choille**..... krok na bren choola [kolly]	Hillock of the Putrid Woodland

Height	Mountain	Translation
348m 1141ft	**Beinn Glas Choire**............ bay-n glas chora [korry]	Hill of the Green Hollow
283m 928ft	**Cnoc na Feadaige**............ krok na fay-da-ga	Hillock of the Whistler
272m 892ft	**Beinn na Coireag**............. bay-n na cor-ak	Hill of the Hollows
269m 882ft	**Cnocan Conachreag**........ krok-an cona-chray-k	Hillock of the Mossy Rocks

21 DORNOCH, ALNESS AND INVERGORDON

Height	Mountain	Translation
692m 2270ft	**Beinn Tharsuinn** .... bay-n [ben] tar-sin	Transverse Hill
546m 1791ft	**Cnoc Muigh Bhlaraidh**..... krok mooy vlar-ay	Hillock of the Plain Moor
523m 1715ft	**Cnoc Cleislein** .... krok kleesh-lin	Hillock of the Herbs
495m 1624m	**Meall an Tuirc** .... me-yal an toork	Hill of Boar
397m 1302ft	**Cnoc Corr Guine** .... krok kor goon-i	Peaked Hillock of Pain
379m 1243ft	**Cnoc an t-Sabhail**............ krok an ta-val [sa-val]	Hillock of the Barn
371m 1217ft	**Struie** .... stroo-i	Wasteland
349m 1145ft	**Beinn Domhuaill**.............. bay-n [ben] don-ool	Donald's Hill
344m 1128ft	**Creag a'Ghobhair** .... kray-k a gour	Peak of the Goats
340m 1115ft	**Cnoc Dubh Mor** .... krok doo more	Big Black Hillock
339m 1112ft	**Cnoc a'Bhreacaich**........... krok a-vrech-ach	Speckled Hillock
321ft 1053ft	**Cnoc an t-Sabhail** .... krok an ta-val [sav-al]	Hillock of the Barn
297m 974ft	**Cnoc a'Choire Bhuidhe**.... krok a cora boo-ya [korry boo-ee]	Hillock of the Yellow Hollow
259m 850ft	**Creag an Amalaidh**.......... kray-k an am-a-lay	Hindrance Rocks
240m 787ft	**Cnoc Navie**....................... krok na-vi	Hostile Hillock

14 Tarbert and Loch Seaforth
(1 Corbett)

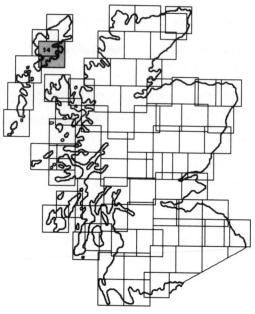

© Crown Copyright

14 TARBERT AND LOCH SEAFORTH

	Height	Mountain	Translation	Map Ref.
○	**799m** 2621ft	**Clisham** klish-am	Rocky Cliff	155073
	743m 2437ft	**Mulla fo Dheas** mool-la fo jess	South Ridge	
	729m 2391ft	**Uisgnaval Mor** u-isg-na-val more	Big Outer Hill	
	697m 2286ft	**Teilesval** teel-es-val	unknown	
	679m 2227ft	**Tirga Mor** tir-ga more	unknown	
	662m 2171ft	**Oreval** or-e-val	Moor Fowl Hill	
	659m 2162ft	**Ullaval** ull-a-val	Wolf Hill	
	614m 2014ft	**Mullach an Langa** mool-lach an lan-ka	The Long Ridge	

Height	Mountain	Translation
579m 1899ft	**Stulaval**.......................... stool-a-val	Enclosure Hill
572m 1876ft	**Carn Ban** .... karn ban	White Hill
572m 1876ft	**Beinn Mhor** .... bay-n [ben] voar	Big Hill
559m 1834ft	**Sgaoth Aird** .... skou ard	High Steep Hill
552m 1811ft	**Tomnaval** .... tom-na-val	unknown
531m 1742ft	**Sgaoth Iosal**.................... skou ees-al	Low Steep Hill
528m 1732ft	**Toddum**........................... tod-dum	unknown
523m 1715ft	**Uisgnaval Beg** .... u-isg-na-val beg	Small Outer Hill
511m 1676ft	**Cleiseval**.......................... klees-e-val	Rocky Hill
506m 1660ft	**Beinn Dhubh** .... bay-n [ben] doo	Black Hill
492m 1614ft	**Liuthaid** .... loo-tat	Numerous
491m 1611ft	**Sron Scourst** .... srawn skoorst	Point of the Valley Crossing a Ridge
486m 1594ft	**Carn Ban** .... karn ban	White Hill
473m 1551ft	**Mullach a'Ruisg** .... mool-lach a rooshk	Bare Summit
471m 1545ft	**Gillaval** .... gill-a-val	Gorge Hill
470m 1542ft	**Gormol**............................ gor-mol	Blue Hill
467m 1532ft	**Ceann Reamhar**............... kyann rav-ar	Fat Head
454m 1489ft	**Muladal** .... mool-a-dal	Promontory Valley
453m 1486ft	**Rapaire**........................... ra-pire	Worthless Fellow
449m 1473ft	**Caiteshal**........................ kate-shal	The Castle
447m 1466ft	**Crionaig** .... kree-on-ak	Little Hill
442m 1450ft	**Sron Ulladale** .... srawn ul-la-dal	Wolf Point
424m 1391ft	**Muaithahal** .... moo-ta-hal	Narrow Hill

Height	Mountain	Translation
401m	**Mor Mhonadh**	Big Moor
1315ft	more mon-ah	
397m	**Beinn Mheadhonach**	Middle Hill
1302ft	bay-n [ben] mee-yon-ach	
389m	**Beinn na h-Uamha**	Hill of the Caves
1276ft	bay-n [ben] na hoo-va	
389m	**Straiaval**	unknown
1276ft	stray-a-val	
378m	**Kearnaval**	unknown
1240ft	keer-na-val	
371m	**Uisenis**	unknown
1217ft	oos-en-is	
370m	**Beinn a'Mhuill**	Hill of the Mound
1214ft	bay-n [ben] a vool	
358m	**Uaval**	unknown
1174ft	oo-a-val	
354m	**Mula Chaolartan**	Narrow Ridge
1161ft	moola choul-ar-tan	
351m	**Beinn a'Deas**	South Hill
1151ft	bay-n [ben] a jess	
349m	**Beinn a'Tuath**	North Hill
1145ft	bay-n [ben] a too-ah	
334m	**Uiseval**	unknown
1096ft	oos-e-val	
328m	**Clett Ard**	High Ridge
1076ft	klett ard	
323m	**Beinn Tharsuinn**	Transverse Hill
1059ft	bay-n [ben] tar-sin	
321m	**Beinn a'Chaolais**	Hill of the Narrows
1056ft	bay-n [ben] a choul-ash	
308m	**Beinn a'Bhoth**	Hill of the Hut
1010ft	bay-n [ben] a bow	

15 Loch Assynt
(2 Munros)
(10 Corbetts)

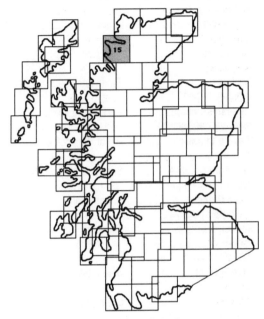

© Crown Copyright

15 LOCH ASSYNT

Height	Mountain	Translation	Map Ref.
❏ 998m 3274ft	**Ben More Assynt** ben more ass-int	Mountain of the Rocky Ridge	318201
❏ 987m 3238ft	**Conival** kon-i-val	Mountain of the Rocks	303199
○ 849m 2785ft	**Cul Mor** kool more	Big Back	162119
○ 846m 2775ft	**Canisp** kan-isp	White Hill	203187
○ 815m 2674ft	**Creag Liath** kray-k lee-ah	Grey Rocks	287158
	Quinag koo-nak Highest peak:	Water Spout	
○ 808m 2651ft	**Sail Gharbh** saal garv	Rough Heel	209292

Height	Mountain	Translation	Map Ref.
○ 801m 2628ft	**Meallan Liath Coire Mhic Dhughaill** me-yal-an lee-ah cora [korry] vik doo-al	Grey Hill of MacDougall's Hollow	357392
○ 792m 2598ft	**Ben Leoid** ben lee-ot	Sloping Hill	320295
○ 776m 2546ft	**Glas Bheinn** glas vay-n [ven]	Green Hill	255265
○ 776m 2546ft	**Sail Gorm** saal gor-om	Blue Heel	198304
○ 769m 2523ft	**Cul Beag** kool bay-k [beg]	Small Back	140088
○ 764m 2506ft	**Spidean Coinnich** speet-yan kon-yeech	Peak of the Moss	205278
750m 2460ft	**Meall a'Chuail** me-yal a choo-al	Hill of the Lock of Hair	
743m 2437ft	**Ben More Coigach** ben more koy-yach	Big Hand-shaped Hill	
742m 2434ft	**Beinn Uidhe** bay-n [ben] oo-ya	Stream Hill	
	Suilven sool-a-ven Highest peak:	The Pillar	
731m 2398ft	**Caistel Liath** kash-tyal lee-ah	Grey Castle	
715m 2345ft	**Breabag** bray-bag	Little Slope	
715m 2345ft	**Meall an Aonaich** me-yal an ou-nach [an-ach]	Hill of the Ridge	
703m 2306ft	**Sgurr an Fhidhleir** skoor an fee-ler	Peak of the Fiddler	
686m 2250ft	**Sgornan Mor** skoor-nan more	Big Peaks	
625m 2050ft	**Breabag Tarsuinn** bray-bag tar-sinn	Little Transverse Hill	
618m 2027ft	**Beinn an Eoin** bay-n [ben] an yawn	Hill of the Bird	
613m 2011ft	**Stac Pollaidh** stak paul-ay	Lumpy Peak	
593m 1945ft	**Cnoc na Creige** krok na kreeka	Rocky Hillock	
588m 1929ft	**Sgorr Tuath** skoor too-ah	North Peak	
578m 1896ft	**Meall an Fhuarainn** me-yal an foor-an	Hill of the Wells	
572m 1876ft	**Beinn Reidh** bay-n [ben] re	Plain Hill	

Height	Mountain	Translation
568m 1863ft	**Beinn nan Cnaimhseag** ... bay-n [ben] kray-shag	Hill of the Black Head
547m 1794ft	**Beinn a'Bhuta** .... bay-n [ben] a voo-ta	Hill of the Snares
546m 1791ft	**An Laogh** .... an lou-ch	The Calf
530m 1738ft	**Beinn Aird da Loch** .... bay-n [ben] ard da loch	Hill of the High Loch
516m 1692ft	**Meall Coire an Lochain** ... me-yal cora [korry] an loch-in	Hill of the Hollow of the High Loch
499m 1637ft	**Beinn an Fhuarain** .... bay-n [ben] an foor-an	Hill of the Wells
421m 1381ft	**Meall a'Bhuirich** .... me-yal a voor-eech	Hill of the Bellowing
408m 1388ft	**Beinn Chroisg** .... bay-n [ben] chroshk	Hill of the Cross
393m 1289ft	**Beannan Beaga** .... bay-nan bayk [bega]	Small Hill
380m 1246ft	**Cnoc an Leathaid** .... krok an lay-hat	Hillock of the Slope
356m 1168ft	**Creag na h-Iolaire** .... kray-k na h-yool-ir	Rock of the Eagle

49

16 Lairg and Loch Shin
(1 Munro)
(2 Corbetts)

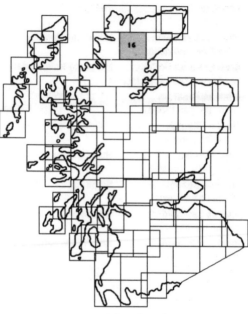

© Crown Copyright

16 LAIRG AND LOCH SHIN

	Height	Mountain	Translation	Map Ref.
❏	**961m** 3153ft	**Ben Klibreck** ben klee-breck	Mountain of the Speckled Cliff	585299
○	**873m** 2863ft	**Ben Hee** ben hee	Fairy Hill	426339
	807m 2647ft	**Creag an Lochain** kray-k an loch-in	Rock of the Little Loch	
○	**801m** 2628ft	**Mellan Liath Coire** **Mhic Dhughaill** me-yal-an lee-ah cora vik doo-al	Grey Hill of MacDougall's Hollow	357392
	796m 2611ft	**Carn Dearg** karn jer-ak	Red Hill	
	774m 2339ft	**Meall an Eoin** me-yal an yawn	Hill of the Bird	
	759m 2490ft	**Carn na Tional** karn na tee-on-al	Hill of the Gathering	

Height	Mountain	Translation
721m 2365ft	**Meall Aileim**.................. me-yal ay-lem	Rocky Hill
713m 2339ft	**Creag Mhor**...................... kray-k voar	Big Rock
704m 2309ft	**Ben Armine**...................... ben ar-min	Weapons Hill
694m 2276ft	**Meall nan Aighean**.......... me-yal nan ay-yan	Hill of the Deer
692m 2270ft	**Creag na h-Iolaire**........... kray-k na h-yool-ir	Eagle Rock
688m 2257ft	**Beinn Direach**.................. bay-n [ben] jeer-ach	Straight Hill
683m 2240ft	**Meall Liath Mor**.............. me-yal lee-ah more	Big Grey Hill
634m 2080ft	**Meall Ard**.......................... me-yal ard	High Hill
628m 2060ft	**Meall a'Chleirich**............. me-yal a chler-eech	Clergyman's Hill
613m 2010ft	**Meall an Fheur Loch**....... me-yal an fer loch	Grassy Hill of the Loch
580m 1902ft	**Meall a'Bhata**.................. me-yal a va-ta	Hill of the Rod
553m 1813ft	**Creag Dhubh Mor**............ kray-k doo more	Big Black Rock
544m 1784ft	**Beinn an Eoin**................... bay-n [ben] an yawn	Hill of the Bird
502m 1551ft	**Meall an Fhuarainn**......... me-yal an foor-an	Hill of the Wells
468m 1535ft	**Creag Dhubh Mor**............ kray-k doo more	Big Black Rock
465m 1525ft	**Creag na Suibheag**.......... kray-k na soo-vay-k	Dogs Tooth Rock
461m 1512ft	**Meallan Liath Mor**........... me-yal-an lee-ah more	Big Grey Hill
435m 1427ft	**Beinn Sgreamhaidh**......... bay-n [ben] skrev-ay	Loathesome Hill
434m 1424ft	**Cnoc an Liath Bhaid** .... **Mhoir** krok an lee-ah vat voar	Big Grey Hillock
402m 1319ft	**Cnoc a'Choire**.................. krok a cora [korry]	Hillock of the Hollow
372m 1220ft	**Cnoc a'Choilich**............... krok a chil-yeech	Hillock of the Cockerel
370m 1214ft	**Meall Eachainn**................. me-yal yach-an	Little Horse Hill

Height	Mountain	Translation
336m	**An Stoc-Bheinn**................	Hill of the Tree Trunk
1102ft	an stok vay-n [ven]	
282m	**Cnoc Bad an Leathaid**	Hillock of the Tufted Meadow
925ft	krok bad an lay-hat	

18 Sound of Harris

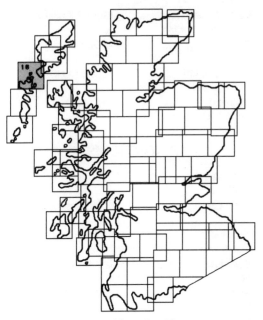

© Crown Copyright

18 HARRIS

Height	Mountain	Translation
506m 1670ft	**Beinn Dhubh** bay-n [ben] doo	Black Hill
460m 1509ft	**Roinebhal** roy-ne-val	Rough Hill
398m 1305ft	**Bleaval** ble-a-val	Butter Hill
386m 1266ft	**An Coileach** an kil-yach	The Cockerel
384m 1260ft	**Heileabhal Mor** heel-a-val more	unknown
374m 1227ft	**Bhoiseabhal** vosh-a-val	unknown
365m 1197ft	**Chaipaval** chap-a-val	Bowl-shaped Hill
354m 1161ft	**Bulabhal** bool-a-val	unknown
280m 918ft	**Greabhal** grey-val	unknown

Height	Mountain	Translation
271m 889ft	**Mula**.................................... mool-a	Bare Hill
265m 869ft	**Bolaval Scarasta** .... bol-a-val skar-as-ta	Skari-Boli's Hill Farm
251m 823ft	**Maodal**.................................. moo-dal	Narrow Hill
236m 774ft	**Clette Dho'uill** .... klett doo-ool	Dougal's Rock
158m 518ft	**Nisabost**............................ nee-a-bost	Headland Farm

18 NORTH UIST

Height	Mountain	Translation
281m 922ft	**South Lee** .... south lee	South Slope
262m 859ft	**North Lee** .... south lee	North Slope
230m 754ft	**Marrival** .... mar-ri-val	Hill of the Mare
217m 718ft	**Ben Aulasary** .... ben all-a-sary	Olaf's Hill Farm
190m 623ft	**Beinn Mhor** .... bay-n [ben] voar	Big Hill
180m 590ft	**Crogary Mor**..................... krog-ary more	Big Cattle Pen
148m 485ft	**Beinn Bhreac** .... bay-n vrechk [ben vreck]	Speckled Hill
140m 459ft	**Uneval**............................... oo-ne-val	Uni's Hill
133m 436ft	**South Clettraval**.............. south klet-ra-val	Rocky Hill of the South
128m 420ft	**North Clettraval** .... north klet-tra-val	Rocky Hill of the North
120m 393ft	**Ben Risary** .... ben ris-ary	Hill of the Brushwood
120m 393ft	**Carra Crom** .... kar-ra krom	Crooked Stones
117m 384ft	**Beinn Riabhach** .... bay-n [ben] ree-vach	Grizzled Hill
101m 331ft	**Beinn Buidhe** .... bay-n boo-ya [ben boo-ee]	Yellow Hill
101m 331ft	**Skealtraval** .... skeel-tra-val	Hill of the Field Hut

19 Gairloch and Ullapool

(12 Munros)
(12 Corbetts)

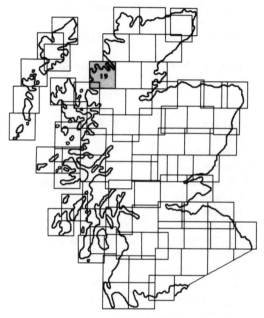

© Crown Copyright

19 GAIRLOCH AND ULLAPOOL

Height	Mountain	Tanslation	Map Ref.
	An Teallach...................... an t-yeel-ach Highest peak:	The Forge	
❑ **1062m** 3484ft	**Bidein a Ghlas Thuill**....... beet-yan a chlas tool	Peak of the Green Hollow .	069843
❑ **1059m** 3474ft	**Sgurr Fiona**...................... skoor fee-on	White Peak	064837
❑ **1019m** 3343ft	**Mullach Coire Mhic** .... **Fhearchair** mool-lach cora [korry] vic feer-char	Hollow Summit of .... the Son of Farquhar	052735
	Beinn Eighe .... bay-n ay-ah [ben ay] Highest peak:	File Mountain	
❑ **1010m** 3313ft	**Ruadh Stac Mor**............... roo-ah stak more	Big Red Peak....................	951611

	Height	Mountain	Translation	Map Ref.
❏	999m 3277ft	A'Chailleach a chal-yach	Old Woman	136714
❏	989m 3245ft	Sgurr Ban skoor ban	White Peak	055745
❏	985m 3232ft	Ben Alligin ben al-li-gin	Jewel Mountain	866613
	981m 3218ft	Sail Mhor saal voar	Big Heel	
	981m 3218ft	Glas Mheall Mor glas ve-yal more	Big Green Hill	
❏	980m 3215ft	Slioch shlee-och	The Spear	005688
	971m 3185ft	Sgurr Ban skoor ban	White Peak	
❏	967m 3127ft	A'Mhaighdean a vay-tyan	The Virgin	008749
	961m 3153ft	Carn na Criche karn na kree-cha	Hill of the Boundary	
	954m 3129ft	Sail Liath saal lee-ah	Grey Heel	
❏	936m 3071ft	Beinn Tarsuinn bayn [ben] tar-sinn	Transverse Mountain	039727
	933m 3060ft	Sgurr an Tuill Bhain skoor an tool van	Peak of the Pale Hollow	
❏	918m 3012ft	Ruadh Stac Mor roo-ah stak more	Big Red Peak	018756
	918m 3012ft	Sgurr Dubh skoor doo	Black Peak	
❏	915m 3000ft	Beinn a'Chlaidheimh bay-n [ben] a chlay-eev	Mountain of the Sword	061775
◯	914m 2998ft	Beinn Dearg bay-n [ben] jer-ak	Red Hill	895608
◯	910m 2988ft	Beinn Dearg Mor bay-n [ben] jer-ak more	Big Red Hill	032799
◯	896m 2940ft	Ruadh Stac Beag roo-ah stak bay-k [beg]	Small Red Peak	973614
◯	881m 2887ft	Meall a'Ghiubhais me-yal a choo-vash	Hill of the Pine Tree	976634
◯	875m 2871ft	Baosbheinn boush-vayn [ven]	Wizard's Hill	871654
◯	860m 2821ft	Beinn Lair bay-n [ben] layer	Hill of the Mare	982732
◯	857m 2812ft	Beinn a'Chaisgein Mor bay-n [ben] a chash-ken more	Big Forbidding Hill	983785
◯	855m 2804ft	Beinn an Eoin bay-n [ben] an yawn	Hill of the Bird	905646

Height	Mountain	Translation	Map Ref.
○ **820m** 2690ft	**Beinn Dearg Bheag**.......... bay-n [ben] jer-ak vay-k [beg]	Little Red Hill....................	020811
○ **807m** 2647ft	**Creag Rainich**.................. kray-k ran-eech	Bracken Rock	097751
○ **791m** 2594ft	**Beinn Airigh Charr**.......... bay-n [ben] arry charr	Hill of the Still Pasture......	930762
○ **767m** 2516ft	**Sail Mhor**........................ saal voar	Big Heel............................	033887
761m 2496ft	**Carn na Feola** .... karn na feela	Hill of the Flesh	
758m 2468ft	**Sgurr Ruadh**...................... skoor roo-ah	Red Peak	
748m 2453ft	**Groban** .... gro-pan	Point of Rock	
739m 2424ft	**An Sguman** .... an skoo-man	The Hollow	
725m 2378ft	**Beinn a'Chearcail**............ bay-n [ben] a cheer-kal	Circular Hill	
720m 2362ft	**Meall Mheinnidh** .... me-yal ven-nay	Hill of Mercy	
711m 2332ft	**Beinn nan Ramh**.............. bay-n [ben] nan rav	Hill of the Oar	
705m 2312ft	**Meall a'Chaorainn**........... me-yal a chou-rann	Hill of the Rowan Tree	
703m 2306ft	**Spidean na Clach** .... speet-yan na klach	Thin Strip of Rock	
702m 2303ft	**Mac is Mathair** .... mak is ma-hir	Mother and Son	
692m 2270ft	**Beinn a'Mhuinidh**............ bay-n [ben] a voon-ay	Hill at the Top	
690m 2263ft	**Meall Chuaich** .... me-yal choo-ach	Bowl-shaped Hill	
680m 2230ft	**Beinn a'Chaisgen Beag** ... bay-n [ben] a chash-ken bay-k [beg]	Small Quiet Hill	
678m 2224ft	**Meall a'Choire Glas** .... me-yal a chora [korry] glas	Hill of the Green Hollow	
668m 2191ft	**Beinn Bheag** .... bay-n vay-k [ben beg]	Little Hill	
635m 2083ft	**Beinn Ghobhlach** .... bay-n [ben] gowl-ach	Forked Hill	
628m 2060ft	**Creag Mheall Mor**........... kray-k ve-yal more	Hill of the Big Rock	

20 Beinn Dearg

(17 Munros)
(7 Corbetts)

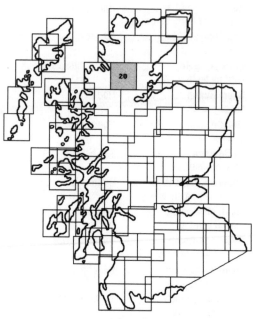

© Crown Copyright

20 BEINN DEARG

Height	Mountain	Translation	Map Ref.
❏ 1110m 3634ft	**Sgurr Mor** skoor more	Big Peak	203718
❏ 1093m 3586ft	**Sgurr na Clach Geala** skoor na klach g-yala	Peak of the White Stones	184715
❏ 1084m 3556ft	**Beinn Dearg** bay-n [ben] jer-ak	Red Mountain	259812
	Ben Wyvis ben wee-vis Highest Peak:	Awesome Mountain	
❏ 1046m 3432ft	**Glas Leathad Mor** glas lay-hat more	Big Green Slope	463684
❏ 1000m 3281ft	**Sgurr Breac** skoor brechk [breck]	Speckled Peak	158711
❏ 999m 3277ft	**A'Chailleach** a chal-yach	The Old Woman	136714

Height	Mountain	Translation	Map Ref.
❏ 980m 3215ft	Cona Mheall .... kona ve-yal	Mountain of the Moss	275816
❏ 977m 3205ft	Meall nan Ceapraichean . me-yal nan k-ya-preech-an	Mountain of the High Top.	257825
955m 3132ft	Tom a'Choinnich .... toom [tom] a chon-yeech	Mound of the Moss	
❏ 954m 3130ft	Beinn Liath Mhor Fannaich bay-n [ben] lee-ah voar fan-nach	Big Grey Mountain of the.. Fannich	219724
❏ 954m 3130ft	Am Faochgach .... am fou-kach	Place of Shells..................	303793
950m 3116ft	An Cabar......................... an ka-bar	The Antler	
❏ 949m 3113ft	Meall Gorm...................... me-yal gor-om	Blue Mountain	221696
❏ 934m 3064ft	Meall a'Chrasgaidh......... me-yal a chra-skay	Mountain of the Crossing.	184733
❏ 933m 3061ft	Fionn Bheinn .... fee-on vay-n [ven]	White Mountain................	147621
❏ 928m 3045ft	Eididh nan Clach Geala ... aid-ye nan klach g-yala	Web of White Stones........	257842
❏ 927m 3041ft	Seana Bhraigh................. she-na vray	Old Upper Part..................	281878
❏ 923m 3028ft	An Coileachan .... an kil-yach-an	Little Cock	241680
❏ 923m 3028ft	Sgurr nan Each .... skoor nan yach	Peak of the Horses	184697
910m 2985ft	Carn Gorm-Toch .... karn gor-om toch	Hill of the Blue Ham	
◯ 889m 2916ft	Beinn Enaiglair................. bayn [ben] en-ak-lar	Hill of the Timid Birds.......	225805
885m 2902ft	Meall Gorm...................... me-yal gor-om	Blue Hill	
882m 2893ft	Meall Ban .... me-yal ban	White Hill	
872m 2860ft	Iorguill .... eer-gool	The Quarrel	
859m 2818ft	Meall Glac an Ruighe...... me-yal glak a roo-ya	Hill of the Arm Grasp	
◯ 845m 2772ft	Carn Ban .... karn ban	White Hill..........................	339875
◯ 838m 2749ft	Carn Chuinneag .... karn choon-ayk	Hill of the Milk Bucket	484833
837m 2745ft	Bodach Beag.................... botach bay-k [beg]	Little Old Man	
822m 2696ft	Bodach Mor .... botach more	Big Old Man	

Height	Mountain	Translation	Map Ref.
○ 807m 2648ft	**Creag Rainich** .... kray-y ran-eech	Bracken Rock	096751
○ 787m 2581ft	**Beinn a'Chaisteil** .... bay-n [ben] a chash-tyal	Hill of the Castle	370801
772m 2532ft	**Meall a'Ghrianain** .... me-yal a chree-an-in	Hill of the Sunny Spot	
○ 764m 2506ft	**Little Wyvis** .... little wee-vis	Little Awesome Mountain.	430645
757m 2483ft	**Creag Dhubh Fannaich** .... kray-k doo fan-nach	Black Rock of the Feeble	
○ 756m 2480ft	**Beinn Liath Mhor a' Ghiubhais Li** bay-n [ben] lee-ah voar choo-vash lee	Big Grey Hill of the .... Colourful Pines	281713
745m 2444ft	**An Socach** .... an soch-ach	The Beak	
742m 2434ft	**Tom Ban Mor** .... toam [tom] ban more	Big White Mound	
742m 2434ft	**Beinn na Eun** .... bay-n [ben] na ayn	Hill of the Bird	
738m 2421ft	**Meall Mor** .... me-yal more	Big Hill	
735m 2411ft	**Carn Loch Sruban Mora**... karn loch sroo-pan mora	Hill of the Clam Loch	
730m 2394ft	**Meall Doire Faid**.............. me-yal dor-ee [dora] faad	Hill of the Lumpy Thicket	
714m 2342ft	**Beinn Tharsuinn** .... bay-n [ben] tar-sinn	Transverse Hill	
706m 2316ft	**Tom na Caillich** .... toam [tom] na kal-yach	Mound of the Old Woman	
704m 2309ft	**Meall na Drochaide**......... me-yal na droch-at	Hill of the Bridge	
701m 2299ft	**Carn a'Choin Deirg** .... karn a choy-n jer-ak	Hill of the Red Dog	
698m 2289ft	**Carn Feur Lochan** .... karn fee-ar loch-an	Hill of the Little Loch with grass	
694m 2276ft	**Carn Loch nan Amhaichean** karn loch nan av-ach-yan	Hill of the Neck-shaped Loch	
691m 2267ft	**Dunan Liath** .... doon-an [dun-an] lee-ah	Grey Fort	
687m 2254ft	**Beinn Dearg**..................... bay-n [ben] jer-ak	Red Hill	
677m 2221ft	**Meall nan Bradhan**.......... me-yal nan bra-tan	Hill of the Salmon	
676m 2250ft	**Meall na Speireig**............ me-yal na speer-ik	Hill of the Sparrow Hawk	

Height	Mountain	Translation
666m 2184ft	**Meall Coire nan Laoigh**... me-yal cora [korry] nan lou-ch	Hill of the Calf's Hollow
665m 2181ft	**Beinn Liath Bheag** .... bay-n [ben] lee-ah vay-k [beg]	Little Grey Hill
657m 2155ft	**Creachan nan Sgadan** ..... kree-ach-an nan ska-tan	Bare Hill of the Herring
648m 2125ft	**Meall Beag** .... me-yal bay-k [beg]	Little Hill
645m 2116ft	**Carn an Lochan**................ karn an loch-an	Hill of the Little Loch
645m 2116ft	**Carn Salachaidh** .... karn sal-ach-ay	Dirty Hill
644m 2113ft	**Sgor a'Chaorainn**............. skoor a chou-ran	Peak of the Rowan Tree
642m 2106ft	**Meall Doo** .... me-yal doo	Black Hill
640m 2099ft	**Carn Mor**.......................... karn more	Big Hill
636m 2086ft	**Carn Alladale**................... karn al-la-dale	Holy Valley Hill
632m 2073ft	**Meall a'Chaorainn**........... me-yal a chou-ran	Hill of the Rowan Tree
628m 2060ft	**Meall a'Chuaille**.............. me-yal choo-il-a	Stake Hill
627m 2057ft	**Carn nan Aighean** .... karn nan ay-yan	Hill of the Hinds
622m 2040ft	**Sron Gun Aran** .... srawn gun aran	Point without Bread
618m 2027ft	**Meall Leacachain**............ me-yal lecht-ach-an	Hill of the Little Slabs

22 Benbecula
31 Barra and surrounding Islands

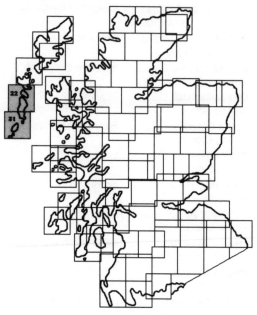

© Crown Copyright

22 BENBECULA

NORTH UIST

Height	Mountain	Translation
347m 1138ft	**Eaval** .... ee-a-val	Isthmus Hill
145m 476ft	**Beinn na h-Aire** .... bay-n [ben] na heera	Hill of the Chicken
140m 459ft	**Burrival** .... burr-i-val	Fortress Hill
115m 377ft	**Beinn a'Charnain** .... bay-n [ben] a charn-in	Stony Hill

BENBECULA

Height	Mountain	Translation
124m 407ft	**Rueval** .... roo-e-val	unknown
102m 335ft	**Beinn Tuath** .... bay-n [ben] too-ah	North Hill

SOUTH UIST

Height	Mountain	Translation
620m 2033ft	**Beinn Mhor** bay-n [ben] voar	Big Hill
606m 1988ft	**Hecla**.................... hek-la	Shrouded Hill
527m 1728ft	**Ben Corodale** .... ben koro-dale	Hill of Koro's Valley
374m 1226ft	**Stulaval**........................... stool-a-val	Milking-shed Hill
257m 843ft	**Ben na Hoe** .... ben na ho	Headland Hill
252m 827ft	**Arnaval** .... ar-na-val	Eagles Hill
223m 731ft	**Sheaval**............................ she-a-val	unknown
196m 643ft	**Trinaval**........................... trin-a-val	unknown
182m 597ft	**Mullach a'Ghlinn Mhoir** .. mool-ach ach-lin voar	Ridge of the Big Glen
181m 594ft	**Layaval** .... lay-a-val	Low Hill
176m 577ft	**Beinn Ghot**....................... bay-n chot	Slanting Hill
170m 557ft	**Beinn Bheag Tuath** .... bay-n vay-k [ben beg] too-ah	Small North Hill
168m 551ft	**Ben Tarbert**...................... ben tar-bert	Isthmus Hill
158m 518ft	**Beinn Shuravat** .... bay-n [ben] shoor-vat	unknown
126m 413ft	**Askervein**......................... ask-er-vin	unknown
120m 394ft	**Criribheinn**....................... kree-ree-ven	unknown

31 BARRA AND SURROUNDING ISLANDS
SOUTH UIST

357m 1171ft	**Triuebheinn** .... troo-ven	unknown
280m 918ft	**Beinn Ruigh Choinnich**.... bayn [ben] rooch chon-yeech	Hill with the Mossy Slope
201m 659ft	**Roneval**............................ ron-e-val	Rough Hill

Height	Mountain	Translation
162m	**Marraval**	Mare's Hill
531ft	mar-ra-val	
122m	**Beinn Oitir**	Low Promontory
400ft	bayn [ben] oy-tir	

ERISKAY

185m	**Ben Scrien**	Scree Hill
607ft	ben scree-en	
122m	**Ben Stack**	Rocky Hill
400ft	ben stack	

BARRA

383m	**Heaval**	Outlying Hill
1256ft	he-a-val	
333m	**Ben Tangaval**	Hill on the Point of Land
1092ft	ben tan-ga-val	
294m	**Grianan**	Sunny Spot
964ft	gree-nan	
245m	**Ben Mhartainn**	Martin's Hill
804ft	ben var-tin	
208m	**Ben Cliad**	Rough Hill
682ft	ben kleed	
200m	**Erival**	Eyri's Hill
656ft	er-i-val	
197m	**Ben Verrisey**	Precipice Hill
646ft	ben ver-ri-say	
183m	**Ben Scute**	Hill of the Spout
600ft	ben skoot	
137m	**Ben Obe**	Hill of the Pool
450ft	ben op-e	

VATERSAY

190m	**Heishival Mor**	unknown
623ft	hesh-i-val more	
169m	**Heishival Beag**	unknown
554ft	hesh-i-val bay-k [beg]	

Terrain typical of the north-west – Map 15 (S. Widdicombe)

An Teallach – Map 19 (G. Cuthbert)

Beinn Alligin, far north – Map 24 (J. Cuthbert)

Liathach, far north – Map 25 (J. Cuthbert)

The Cuillins, Isle of Skye – Map 32 (S. Widdicombe)

*Lunch break on the Buachaille Etive Mor, Glencoe – Map 41
(J. Cuthbert)*

Stob Dearg, Glencoe – Map 41 (G. Cuthbert)

Scrambling in the Lost Valley, Glencoe – Map 41 (J. Cuthbert)

Bidean nam Bian from Aonach Eagach, Glencoe – Map 41
(J. Cuthbert)

View from Glencoe to Loch Rannoch in the background – Map 41
(J. Cuthbert)

Glencoe from Aonach Eagach – Map 41 (J. Cuthbert)

24 Raasay, Applecross, Loch Torridon
(1 Munro)
(4 Corbetts)

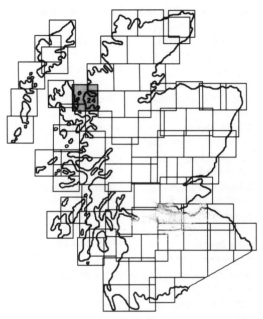

© Crown Copyright

24 RAASAY, APPLECROSS, LOCH TORRIDON

	Height	Mountain	Translation	Map Ref.
❑	**985m** 3231ft	**Beinn Alligin** bay-n [ben] al-li-gin	Jewel Mountain	866613
	922m 3024ft	**Tom na Gruagaich** toam [tom] na groo-yach	Mound of the Maiden	
○	**914m** 2998ft	**Beinn Dearg** bay-n [ben] jer-ak	Red Hill	895608
○	**902m** 2959ft	**Beinn Damh** bay-n [ben] dav	Hill of the Stag	893502
○	**896m** 2939ft	**Beinn Bhan** bay-n [ben] van	White Hill	804450
○	**776m** 2545ft	**Sgurr a'Chaorachain** skoor a chou-rach-an	Peak of the Rowan Berries	797417
	739m 2424ft	**Creag an Fhitich** kray-k an fee-teech	Rock of the Raven	

Height	Mountain	Translation
715m 2345ft	**Beinn an Eoin** .... bay-n [ben] an yawn	Hill of the Bird
712m 2335ft	**Coire Gorm Beag** .... cora [korry] gor-om bay-k [beg]	Small Blue Hollow
710m 2329ft	**Meall Gorm** .... me-yal gor-om	Blue Hill
687m 2253ft	**Sgurr na Bana Mhoraire** .. skoor na bana voar-ayr	Peak of the Countess
672m 2204ft	**An Ruadh-Mheallan** .... an roo-ah ve-yal-an	The Red Hill
646m 2119m	**Carn Dearg** .... karn jer-ak	Red Hill
626m 2053ft	**Meall an Doireachan** .... me-yal an dor-ach-an	Hill of the Thickets
624m 2047ft	**Bheinn Bhreac** .... vay-n vrech-t [ven vrek]	Speckled Hill
533m 1748m	**Ben Sheildaig** .... ben sheel-dig	Meadow Hill
518m 1699ft	**Mheall na Fhuaid** .... ve-yal na food	Hill of the Scarecrow
513m 1683m	**Beinn na Chait** .... bay-n [ben] na chat	Hill of the Cat
494m 1620ft	**Croic Bheinn** .... kroy-k vay-n [ven]	Hill of the Deer Antler
442m 1449ft	**Meall na Meine** .... me-yal na men	Hill of the Mine
395m 1296ft	**Bad a'Chreamha** .... bad a chre-va	Cluster of Garlic
392m 1286ft	**Sithean Bhealaich** .... **Chumhaing** sheen ve-yal-ach choo-an	Narrow Peaceful Gorge
321m 1283ft	**Meall Ailein** .... me-yal al-en	Plain Hill
294m 964m	**Mullach nan Cadhaichean** mool-lach nan ka-yach-yan	Summit of the Narrow Path
254m 833ft	**Beinn na h-Iolaire** .... bay-n [ben] na h-yool-ir	Hill of the Eagle

25 Glen Carron

(30 Munros)
(19 Corbetts)

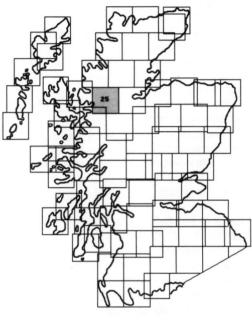

© Crown Copyright

25 GLEN CARRON

	Height	Mountain	Translation	Map Ref.
❏	**1183m** 3881ft	**Carn Eighe** .... karn ay-ah [ay]	File Mountain....................	123262
❏	**1180m** 3871ft	**Mam Sodhail** .... mam sool	Hill of the Barn	120253
❏	**1151m** 3776ft	**Sgurr nan Ceatheamhnan** skoor nan ker-oa-van	Peak of the Quadrant........	057228
❏	**1150m** 3772ft	**Sgurr na Lapaich** .... skoor na laf-eech	Peak of the Bog	161351
	1148m 3765ft	**Stob a'Choire Dhomhainn** stop a chora [korry] do-vin	Peak of the Deep Hollow	
❏	**1129m** 3704ft	**An Riabhachan** .... an ree-vach-an	The Grizzled One	134345
❏	**1111m** 3645ft	**Tom a'Choinnich** .... toam [tom] a chon-yeech	Mountain of the Moss	163273

Height	Mountain	Translation	Map Ref.
❑ **1083m** 3553ft	**Sgurr a'Choire Ghlais**...... skoor a cora [korry] chlash	Peak of the Grey Hollow ...	259430
1074m 3522ft	**Stuc Bheag** .... stook vay-k [beg]	Small Peak	
❑ **1069m** 3507ft	**An Socach**........................ an soch-ach	The Beak...........................	100333
1056m 3464ft	**Coire nan Each** .... cora [korry] nan yach	Hollow of the Horses	
	Liathach........................... lee-ach Highest peak:	The Grey One	
❑ **1054m** 3458ft	**Spidean a'Choire Leith** ... speet-yan a cora [korry] lay	Peak of the Half Hollow	929579
❑ **1054m** 3458ft	**Toll Creagach** .... toll kray-kach	Rocky Hollow	194283
❑ **1053m** 3455ft	**Sgurr a'Chaorachain** .... skoor a chou-rach-an	Peak of the Rowan Tree....	087447
❑ **1049m** 3441ft	**Sgurr Fhurr-t'Huill**........... skoor foor-hoo-il	Peak of the Cold Hollow ...	236437
1046m 3431ft	**Bidean an Eoin Deirg**....... beet-yan an yawn jer-ak	Peak of the Red Birds	
1036m 3398ft	**Sgurr na Lapaich** .... skoor na laf-eech	Peak of Bog	
1030m 3378ft	**Creag Ghorm a'Bhealaich** kray-k chor-om a ve-yal-ach	Blue Rock of the Pass	
❑ **1023m** 3356ft	**Mullach an Rathain**......... mool-lach an raa-han	Summit of the Row .... of Pinnacles	912577
1015m 3329ft	**Sgurr na Feastaig** .... skoor na fee-stak	Peak of the Sea Thrift	
	Beinn Eighe .... bay-n ay-a [ben ay] Highest peak :	File Mountain	
❑ **1010m** 3313ft	**Ruadh Stac Mor**.............. roo-ah stak more	Big Red Peak	951611
❑ **1007m** 3304ft	**Maoile Lunndaidh** .... moula loon-day	Bare Wet Hill	135458
❑ **1005m** 3297ft	**Beinn Fhionnlaidh** .... bay-n [ben] fee-on-lay	Findlay's Mountain	115282
❑ **999m** 3277ft	**Sgurr Choinnich**.............. skoor chon-yeech	Peak of the Moss..............	076446
996m 3266ft	**Carn nam Fiaclan** .... karn nam fee-klan	Hill of the Teeth	
❑ **993m** 3258ft	**Sgurr na Ruaidhe** .... skoor na roo-ah	Peak of the Redness.........	289425
❑ **992m** 3255ft	**Carn nan Gobhar**.............. karn nan gour	Mountain of the Goats......	273439

	Height	Mountain	Translation	Map Ref.
❑	992m 3255ft	**Carn nan Gobhar**.............. karn nan gour	Mountain of the Goats......	182344
❑	986m 3235ft	**Lurg Mhor** .... loork voar	Big Ridge..........................	065405
	983m 3225ft	**Stob a' Choire Liath Mhor** stop a chora [korry] lee-ah voar	Big Peak of the Grey Hollow	
❑	982m 3222ft	**Mullach na Dheiragain**.... mool-ach na yer-a-kan	Summit of the Hawk.........	081259
	971m 3185ft	**Meall Mhor** .... me-yal voar	Big Hill	
	971m 3185ft	**Sgurr Ban**......................... skoor ban	White Peak	
❑	960m 3150ft	**Sgurr Ruadh**...................... skoor roo-ah	Red Peak	959504
	946m 3102ft	**Creag Dubh**...................... kray-k doo	Black Rock	
❑	945m 3100ft	**Bidein a'Choire** .... **Sheasgaich** beet-yan a cora [korry] shees-kach	Peak of the Hollow of the Dry Cattle	049413
❑	933m 3061ft	**Maol Chean Dearg**.......... moul chyan jer-ak	Bald Red Head..................	924498
❑	933m 3061ft	**Fionn Bheinn** .... fee-on vay-n [ven]	White Mountain................	147621
❑	928m 3044ft	**Moruisg**............................ more-ooshk	Big Water	101499
	927m 3040ft	**Am Fasarinenn** .... am faa-sar-in	The Pathway	
❑	925m 3035ft	**Beinn Liath Mhor**............ bay-n [ben] lee-ah voar	Big Grey Mountain............	964519
❑	920m 3018ft	**An Socach**........................ an soch-ach	The Beak..........................	088230
	918m 3011ft	**A'Ghlas Bheinn**................ a chlas vay-n [ven]	The Green Mountain	
	917m 3007ft	**Stob a Choire Lochain**..... stop a chora [korry] loch-in	Peak of the Hollow of the Little Loch	
❑	915m 3001ft	**Sgurr nan Ceannaichean**. skoor nan k-yan-nach-an	Peak of the Pedlars...........	087480
○	914m 2998ft	**Beinn Dearg**..................... bay-n [ben] jer-ak	Red Hill.............................	895608
○	907m 2976ft	**Fuar Tholl** .... foor holl	Cold Hole..........................	975489
○	902m 2959ft	**Beinn Damh** .... bay-n dav	Stag Hill............................	893502
○	899m 2949ft	**Aonach Buidhe** .... ou-nach boo-ya [an-ach boo-ee]	Yellow Ridge	058324

Height	Mountain	Translation	Map Ref.
○ 892m 2926ft	**An Ruadh Stac** .... an roo-ah stak	The Red Pillar	922481
891m 2922ft	**Sgurr na Muice** .... skoor na moo-ka	Peak of the Pigs	
○ 889m 2917ft	**Aonach Shassuinn** .... ou-nach [an-ach] saa-sin	Englishman's Ridge..........	173180
○ 879m 2884ft	**Sguman Choinnich** .... skoo-man chon-yeech	Peak of the Moss.............	977304
○ 879m 2884ft	**Sgurr a'Mhuilinn** .... skoor a voo-linn	Peak of the Mill...............	265558
878m 2880ft	**Sgurr a'Choire Ghairbh** ... skoor a chora [korry] charv	Peak of the Rough Hollow	
875m 2870ft	**Carn Gorm** .... karn gor-om	Blue Hill	
○ 873m 2864ft	**Sgurr nan Lochan Uaine**.. skoor na loch-an oo-ayn	Peak of the Little Green .... Loch	969532
870m 2854ft	**An Creachal Beag**............ an kray-chal bay-k [beg]	Little Bare Summit	
○ 868m 2848ft	**Faochaig** .... fouch-ag	The Whelk	022317
○ 863m 2830ft	**Beinn Tharsuinn** .... bayn [ben] tar-sinn	Transverse Hill	055433
○ 863m 2831ft	**Carn a'Choire Chairbh**..... karn a chora [korru] charv	Hill of the Hollow .... of the Carcass	137189
○ 862m 2827ft	**Sgurr na Feartaig** .... skoor na feer-tag	Peak of the Sea Thrift	055454
861m 2824ft	**Creag Dubh**...................... kray-k doo	Black Rock	
857m 2811ft	**Carn Liath** .... karn lee-ah	Grey Hill	
856m 2808ft	**Creag Ghlas**..................... kray-k chlas	Green Rock	
854m 2801ft	**Creag Dhubh Mhor** .... kray-k doo voar	Big Black Rock	
854m 2801ft	**Garbh Charn**..................... garv charn	Rough Hill	
○ 849m 2785ft	**Bac an Eich**...................... bak an ech	Bank of the Horse.............	222489
844m 2768ft	**Sgurr a'Ghlas Leathaid** ... skoor a chlas lay-hat	Green Sloping Peak	
○ 840m 2755ft	**Meallan na Uan** .... me-yal-an na oo-an	Hill of the Lamb................	264545
○ 818m 2684ft	**Sgorr na Diollaid** .... skoor na jeel-at	Peak of the Saddle...........	282362
○ 814m 2670ft	**An Sidhean** .... an shee-yan	The Fairy Hillock...............	171454

Height	Mountain	Translation	Map Ref.
○ 797m 2615ft	Beinn Dronaig................. bay-n [ben] dron-ak	Hill of the Cushion............	037382
792m 2598ft	Mullach a'Ghlas-Thuill.... mool-lach a chlas hoo-il	Summit of the Green Hollow	
○ 782m 2565ft	Sgurr Dubh....................... skoor doo	Black Peak........................	979558
775m 2542ft	Meall na Faire .... me-yal na fara	Hill of the Skyline	
771m 2529ft	Sail Riabhach .... saal ree-vach	Grizzled Heel	
771m 2529ft	Carn Glas Lochdaroch ..... karn glas loch-dar-och	Hill of the Little Grey Loch	
761m 2496ft	Mullach na Maoile .... mool-lach na moula	Bare Summit	
753m 2470ft	Ben Killilan...................... ben kill-ilan	Church Hill	
737m 2417ft	Beinn na h-Eaglaise .... bayn [ben] a heg-lish	Hill of the Church	
730m 2394ft	Carnan Cruithneachd....... karn-nan kroon-yach-t	Creation Cairn	
715m 2345ft	Carn Loch na Gobhlaig.... karn loch na gow-al-ak	Hill of the Forked Loch	
711m 2332ft	Coire na Feithe Seilich.... korry [cora] na feeth shel-ch	Hollow of the Bog Monster	
711m 2332ft	Glas Bheinn .... glas vay-n [ven]	Green Hill	
706m 2315ft	An Cruachan .... an kroo-ach-an	The Stack	
702m 2302ft	Beinn Bhuide .... bay-n voo-ya [ben voo-ee]	Yellow Hill	
694m 2276ft	Meall Mor .... me-yal more	Big Hill	
694m 2276ft	Mealla Odhar................... me-yala oh-er	Dappled Hill	
693m 2273ft	Beinn na Muice................ bay-n [ben] na moo-ka	Hill of the Pigs	
690m 2263ft	Eagan............................... ay-kan	The Notches	
689m 2260ft	Meall Dubh na Caoidhe... me-yal doo na kou-ya	Hill of the Black Lament	
679m 2227ft	An Soutar......................... an soo-tar	The Shoemaker	
678m 2224ft	Carn Breac .... karn brech-t [brek]	Speckled Hill	
678m 2224ft	Carn na Breabaig............. karn na bray-bag	Hill of the Small Peak	

71

Height	Mountain	Translation
663m 2175ft	**Beinn Mheadhoin** .... bay-n [ben] vee-yon	Middle Hill
661m 2168ft	**Creag nan Calman** .... kray-k nan kal-a-man	Rock of the Doves
657m 2155ft	**Sgurr na h-Eighe** .... skoor na hay-ah	The File Peak
654m 2145ft	**Carn an Alltain Riabhaich** karn an all-tan ree-vach	Hill of the Grizzled Stream
653m 2142ft	**Am Meallan** .... am me-yal-lan	The Hill
642m 2106ft	**Creag a'Ghlastail** .... kray-k a chlash-tal	The Greyish Rock
634m 2080ft	**Carn bad Chreamha** .... karn bad chra-va	Hill of the Wild Garlic Clump
627m 2057ft	**Creag Dhubh Bheag** .... kray-k doo vay-k [beg]	Little Black Rock
625m 2050ft	**Carn an Daimh Bhain** ...... karn an dav van	Hill of the White Stag
619m 2030ft	**Beinn Bheag** .... bay-n vay-k [ben beg]	Little Hill
612m 2007ft	**Creag Dhubh Mhor** .... kray-k doo voar	Big Black Rock

26 Inverness and Strathglass
(1 Corbett)

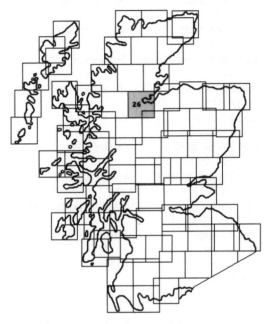

© Crown Copyright

26 INVERNESS AND STRATHGLASS

Height	Mountain	Translation	Map Ref.
○ 862m 2828ft	**Beinn a'Bha'ach Ard**........ bay-n [ben] a vach art	Hill of the High Barn	361435
736m 2415ft	**Carn Ban** .... karn ban	White Hill	
727m 2385m	**Sgurr a'Ghlaisien** .... skoor a chlash-en	Greenish Peak	
714m 2342ft	**Carn na Saobhaidh** .... karn na sou-vay	Hill of the Fox's Den	
711m 2332ft	**Beinn Bhuidhe** .... bay-n voo-ya [ven voo-ee]	Yellow Hill	
696m 2283ft	**Meall Fuar Mhonaidh** ...... me-yal foor von-ay	Hill of the Cold Moor	
683m 2240ft	**Meall a'Mhadaidh** .... me-yal a va-tay	Hill of the Fox	
682m 2237ft	**Beinn Acha'Bhraghad** ...... bay-n [ben] ach a vrach-at	Hill of the Upper Part	

Height	Mountain	Translation
676m 2217ft	**Carn Gorm** .... karn gor-om	Blue Hill
673m 2207ft	**Carn na Coinnich** .... karn na kon-yeech	Hill of the Moss
671m 2201ft	**Meall nan Damh** .... me-yal nan dav	Hill of the Stags
663m 2175ft	**Carn Odhar** .... karn oh-er	Dappled Hill
662m 2171ft	**Meall Guibhais** .... me-yal goo-vash	Hill of the Pines
662m 2171ft	**Carn a'Mhuilt** .... karn a voolt	Hill of Sheep
651m 2135ft	**Glas Bheinn Mhor** .... glas vay-n [ven] voar	Big Green Hill
632m 2073ft	**Carn Doire na h-Achlais** karn dor-ee [dora] na hach-lash	Hill of the Thicket Hollow
631m 2070ft	**Carn Glac an Eich** .... karn glak an ech	Hill of the Horse's Hollow
617m 2024ft	**Carn Tarsuinn** .... karn tar-sinn	Transverse Hill
613m 2011ft	**Carn na Ruighe Duibhe** ... karn nan roo-ah doo	Reddish Black Hill
536m 1758ft	**Creag Loch nan Dearcag** kray-k loch nan jark	Rocky Loch of the Berries
510m 1673ft	**Creag a'Chliabhain** .... kray-k a chlee-vin	Basket Rock
501m 1643ft	**Carn a'Bhodaich** .... karn a votach	Hill of the Old Man
465m 1525ft	**Meall na h-Eilrig** .... me-yal na heel-rik	Hill of the Deer Trap
464m 1522ft	**Tom Bailgean** .... toam [tom] bal-eg-an	Spotted Mound
458m 1502ft	**Carn na Cre** .... karn na kree	Hill of Clay
457m 1499ft	**Carn nan Bad** .... karn nan bad	Hill of the Tufts
457m 1499ft	**Beinn a'Rubha Riabhaich** bayn [ben] a roo-va ree-vach	Hill of the Grizzled Bristle
451m 1479ft	**Meall a'Ghuirmein** .... me-yal a choor-men	Hill of Blueness
446m 1463ft	**Stac na Cathaig** .... stak na ka-tak	Peak of the Warrior
430m 1410m	**Stac Gorm** .... stak gor-om	Blue Peak
418m 1404m	**Meall nan Caorach** .... me-yal nan kou-rach	Hill of the Sheep

Height	Mountain	Translation
414m 1358ft	**An Leacainn** an lech-tan	The Forehead
403m 1355ft	**Carn na Gearraig** karn na g-yar-ak	Hill of the Young Hare
402m 1351ft	**Meall Mor** me-yal more	Big Hill
394m 1292ft	**Cul Mor** kool more	Big Back
370m 1214ft	**Carn Faire na Con** karn fera na kon	Hill with a Watcher
365m 1197ft	**Creag a'Chlachain** kray-k a chlach-in	Rock of the Village
336m 1102ft	**Creag Innis an Daimh Dhuibh** kray-k ee-nish an dav doo	Black Rock on the Deer Meadow

27 Nairn and Forres
28 Elgin and Dufftown
(1 Corbett)

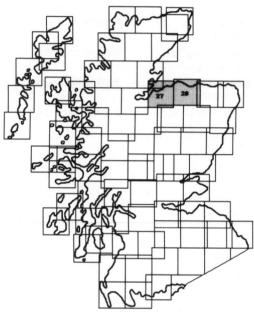

© Crown Copyright

27 NAIRN AND FORRES

Height	Mountain	Translation
616m 2020ft	**Carn na h-Easgainn** .... karn na hesh-kan	Hill of the Eels
615m 2017ft	**Carn nan Tri-Tighernan** ... karn nan tree teer-nan	Hill of the Three Lairds
549m 1801ft	**Carn an Loine** .... karn an loy-n	Hill of the Glade
504m 1653ft	**Craig Ealraich** .... kray-k el-rach	Rock of Burden
492m 1614ft	**Meall Mor** .... me-yal more	Big Hill
486m 1594ft	**Craig Tiribeg** .... kray-k teer-beg	Little Land Rock
485m 1591ft	**Cam Sgriob** .... kam skreeb	Crooked Scrape

Height	Mountain	Translation	Map Ref.
450m 1476ft	**Creag Liath** .... kray-k lee-ah	Grey Rocks	
426m 1397ft	**Tom na Slaite** .... toam [tom] na slat	Mound of the Rod	
417m 1368ft	**Carn Sgumain**.................. karn skoo-man	Hill of the Dish	
371m 1217ft	**Mill Buie** .... meel boo-ee	Yellow Honey	
294m 964ft	**Dundavie**.......................... doon-dav-i	Fort of the Stags	
259m 850ft	**Lethen Bar** .... lay-en bar	Half Summit	

28 ELGIN AND DUFFTOWN

	Height	Mountain	Translation	Map Ref.
○	**840m** 2756ft	**Ben Rinnes** .... ben reen-esh	Headland Hill	255353
	569m 1866ft	**Meikle Conval**.................. me-kil kon-val	Big Mossy Hill	
	552m 1811ft	**Little Conval** .... little kon-val	Little Mossy Hill	
	523m 1715ft	**Hill of Clais na Earb** .... hill of clash na erb	Hill of the Roe Deer Trench	
	471m 1545ft	**Ben Aigan** .... ben egg-an	Near Hill	
	417m 1368ft	**Carran Hill** .... kar-an hill	Shrimp Hill	
	404m 1325ft	**Carn na Cailliche**............. karn na kayl-yeech	Hill of the Old Woman	

23 North Skye
32 South Skye
(12 Munros)
(2 Corbetts)

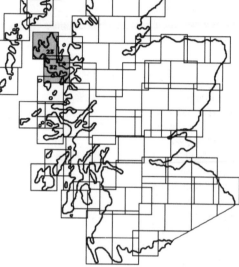

© Crown Copyright

32 SOUTH SKYE

	Height	Mountain	Translation	Map Ref.
❑	**993m** 3258ft	**Sgurr Alasdair** skoor al-a-stir	Alexander's Peak	449208
❑	**986m** 3235ft	**Sgurr Dearg** skoor jer-ak	Red Peak	444215
❑	**973m** 3192ft	**Sgurr a'Ghreadaidh** skoor a chray-tay	Peak of Torment	445232
❑	**965m** 3166ft	**Sgurr na Banachdich** skoor na ba-nach-teech	Peak of the Milkmaid	440225
❑	**965m** 3166ft	**Sgurr nan Gillean** skoor nan geel-yan	Peak of the Young Men	472253
❑	**958m** 3143ft	**Bruach an Frithe** broo-ach an free	Slope of the Deer Forest	461252
❑	**948m** 3110ft	**Sgurr MhicChoinnich** skoor vik-choyn-yeech	Mackenzie's Peak	450210

Height	Mountain	Translation	Map Ref.
947m 3106ft	**Sgurr Sgumain**................. skoor skoo-man	Peak of the Boat Bailer	
❏ 944m 3097ft	**Sgurr Dubh Mor** .... skoor doo more	Big Black Peak..................	457205
❏ 935m 3068ft	**Am Basteir**....................... am baa-stir	Obscure Mountain............	465253
930m 3056ft	**Sgurr a'Fionn Choire** .... skoor a fee-on chora [korry]	Peak of the White Hollow	
❏ 928m 3045ft	**Bla Bheinn** .... bla vay-n [blaven]	Blue Mountain	530217
❏ 924m 3031ft	**Sgurr nan Eag** .... skoor nan ayk	Peak of the Notches	457195
❏ 918m 3012ft	**Sgurr Mhadaidh**.............. skoor va-tay	Peak of the Fox.................	446235
879m 2883ft	**Sgurr Thuilm**.................... skoor hool-m	Peak of the Hillock	
861m 2824ft	**Sgurr na Bhairnich** .... skoor na var-neech	Peak of the Bellowing	
○ 806m 2644ft	**Garbh Bheinn**................... garv vay-n [ven]	Rough Hill	531232
○ 775m 2542ft	**Glamaig** .... glam-ig	Greedy Woman.................	514300
736m 2414ft	**Marsco**............................ mar-sco	Seagull Rock	
732m 2401ft	**Beinn na Caillich** .... bay-n [ben] na kal-yeech	Hill of the Old Woman	
709m 2326ft	**Beinn Dearg Mhor** .... bay-n [ben] jer-ak voar	Big Red Hill	
631m 2070ft	**Sgurr nan Gobhar** .... skoor nan gour	Peak of the Goats	
584m 1916ft	**Beinn Dearg Bheag**......... bay-n [ben] jer-ak vay-k	Little Red Hill	
570m 1870ft	**Glas Bheinn Mhor**........... glas vay-n [ben] voar	Big Grey Hill	
497m 1630ft	**Sgurr na Stri** .... skoor na stree	Peak of Strife	
445m 1460ft	**Ben Lee**........................... ben lee	Sloping Hill	
445m 1460ft	**Beinn Bhreac** .... bay-n vre-chk [ben breck]	Speckled Hill	
436m 1430ft	**Rioneval** .... re-on-e-val	Rough Hill	
435m 1427ft	**An Cruachan** .... an kroo-ach-an	The Stack	
413m 1355ft	**Truagh Mheall** .... trooch ve-yal	Sad Hill	

Height	Mountain	Translation
407m 1335ft	**Am Mam** .... am mam	The Breast
401m 1315ft	**Beinn na Gaoithe** .... bay-n [ben] na gou-ee	Hill of the Wind
400m 1313ft	**Stroc-Bheinn** .... stroch-vay-n [ven]	Ragged Hill
383m 1256ft	**Biod Mor** .... beed more	Big Top
370m 1214ft	**Beinn Bhreac** .... bay-n vre-chk [ben breck]	Speckled Hill
336m 1102ft	**Meall Odhar Mor** .... me-yal oh-er more	Big Dappled Hill
319m 1046ft	**Beinn an Eoin** .... bay-n [ben] an yawn	Hill of the Bird

23 NORTH SKYE

Height	Mountain	Translation
719m 2358ft	**The Storr** .... the stoor	The Peak
668m 2191ft	**Hartaval** .... har-ta-val	Rocky Hill
611m 2004ft	**Beinn Edra** .... bay-n [ben] ed-ra	Outer Hill
607m 1991ft	**Creag a'Lain** .... kray-k a laan	Cornyard Rock
579m 1899ft	**Bealach Mhoramhainn** .... byal-ach voar-av-an	Big Mountain Pass
562m 1843ft	**Ben Dearg** .... ben jer-ak	Red Hill
543m 1781ft	**Meall na Suiramach** .... me-yal na soor-a-mach	Hill of the Sea-nymph
492m 1614ft	**Sgurr Mor** .... skoor more	Big Peak
488m 1601ft	**Healabhal Beag** .... heel-a-val bay-k [beg]	Little Flagstone Hill
485m 1591ft	**Beinn Meadhonach** .... bay-n [ben] mee-yon-ach	Middle Hill
475m 1558ft	**Beinn an Laoigh** .... bay-n [ben] na lou-ch	Hill of the Calf
468m 1535ft	**Healabhal Mhor** .... heel-a-val voar	Big Flagstone Hill
466m 1528ft	**Bioda Buidhe** .... beeda boo-ya [boo-ee]	Yellow Pointed Top
459m 1506ft	**A'Chorra Bheinn** .... a chora-ven	Hill of the Hollow

Height	Mountain	Translation
423m 1387ft	**Beinn Fhuar** .... bay-n [ben] foor	Cold Hill
413m 1355ft	**Ben Tianavaig**.................. ben tee-na-vayk	Peak of the Bay
408m 1338ft	**Beinn Bhac-Ghlas**............ bay-n vach-chlas [ben vach glas]	Hill of the Green Bank
407m 1335ft	**Beinn a'Chapuill**.............. bay-n [ben] a cha-fool	Hill of the Horse
396m 1299ft	**Skriaig** .... skray-k	The Skull
395m 1296ft	**Bealach a'Chaol-reidh**..... b-yal-ach a choul-ree	Slim Pass of the Plain
392m 1286ft	**Sithean Bhealaich** .... **Chumhaing** shee-yan vyal-ach choo-vang	Fairy Hillock of the Narrow Pass
388m 1273ft	**Greagalain**....................... gray-ka-lan	The Donkey
371m 1217ft	**Beinn na Boineid** .... bay-n [ben] na bon-eej	Hill of the Bonnet
350m 1148ft	**Suidh'a Mhinn** .... soo-ya vin	Smooth Seat
348m 1141ft	**Beinn Chapuill** .... bay-n [ben] cha-fool	Hill of the Horses
331m 1086ft	**Beinn Uisga** .... bay-n [ben] oosh-ka	Water Hill
327m 1073ft	**Creag a'Ghuail**................. kray-k a choo-il	Shoulder Rock
324m 1063ft	**Beinn Coinnich** .... bay-n [ben] kon-yeech	Moss Hill
319m 1046ft	**Beinn Mheadhonach**........ bay-n [ben] vee-yon-ach	Middle Hill
318m 1043ft	**Beinn na Boineide** .... bay-n [ben] na bon-eeja	Hill of the Bonnets
314m 1030	**Beinn Bhreac** .... bay-n vrechk [ben breck]	Speckled Hill
310m 1016ft	**Bhealaich Chumhaing** ..... ve-yal-ach choo-vang	Narrow Pass

33 Loch Alsh and Glen Shiel
(36 Munros)
(20 Corbetts)

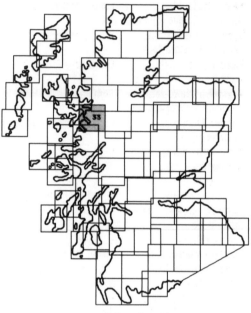

© Crown Copyright

33 LOCH ALSH AND GLEN SHIEL

Height	Mountain	Translation	Map Ref.
❑ 1151m 3776ft	**Sgurr nan Ceathreamhnan** skoor nan ker-oa-nan	Peak of the Quadrant........	057228
❑ 1120m 3674ft	**A'Chralaig**........................ a chral-ak	The Basket........................	094148
❑ 1108m 3634ft	**Meall a'Bhuiridh**.............. me-yal a voor-ee	Mountain of the Bellowing	251502
❑ 1102m 3615ft	**Mullach Fraoch Choire** .... mool-lach frouch chora [korry]	Summit of the Heather .... Hollow	095171
❑ 1100m 3610ft	**Creise** .... kreesh	Fat Lump	238507
❑ 1068m 3504ft	**Sgurr Fhuarain**................. skoor foor-an	Peak of the Cold Well	978167
❑ 1040m 3415ft	**Sgurr na Ciche** .... skoor na keesh-ta	Peak of the Breast	902966

82

Height	Mountain	Translation	Map Ref.
❑ 1038m 3405ft	Sgurr a'Bhealaich Dheirg skoor a ve-yal-ach jer-ak	Peak of the Red Pass........	035143
❑ 1035m 3396ft	Gleouraich .... glaw-reech	Hill of Noise......................	039054
❑ 1032m 3386ft	Beinn Fhada .... bay-n [ben] fata	Long Mountain	018192
❑ 1027m 3369ft	Sgurr na Ciste Duibhe ..... skoor na keesta doo	Peak of the Black Chest	984149
❑ 1027m 3369ft	Sgurr a'Mhaoraich........... skoor a vour-eech	Peak of the Shellfish.........	984065
❑ 1021m 3350ft	Aonach air Chrith............. ou-nach [an-ach] ar chree	Trembling Ridge...............	051083
❑ 1020m 3346ft	Ladhair Bheinn .... lay-ar vay-n [ven]	Claw Mountain	824040
❑ 1013m 3323ft	Garbh Chioch Mor............ garv chee-och more	Big Rough Breast	909961
❑ 1010m 3314ft	The Saddle 	....	936131
❑ 1010m 3314ft	Sgurr an Doire Leathain.. skoor an dor-ee [dora] lay-han	Peak of the Broad Thicket	015099
1008m 3306ft	Coire na Cralaig .... cora [korry] na kral-ik	Hollow of the Basket	
❑ 1004m 3293ft	Sgurr an Lochain .... skoor an loch-in	Peak of the Little Loch......	005104
❑ 1003m 3291ft	Aonach Meadhoin........... ou-nach [an-ach] mee-yon	Middle Mountain	049137
❑ 1003m 3291ft	Sgurr Mor....................... skoor more	Big Peak	965980
1002m 3286ft	Sgurr na Carnach............ skoor na karn-ach	Peak of the Cairns	
❑ 996m 3267ft	Spidean Mialach .... speet-yan meel-ach	Lousy Peak......................	066043
990m 3247ft	Sgurr nan Spainteach...... skoor nan span-t-yach	Peak of the Spaniards	
988m 3241ft	Sgurr an Fhurail .... skoor an foor-il	Peak of the Cold Hollow	
❑ 987m 3238ft	Druim Shionnach............. droom [drim] she-an-nach	Ridge of the Fox	074085
❑ 982m 3222ft	Mullach na Dheiragain.... mool-lach na yer-ak-an	Summit of the Hawk.........	081259
❑ 982m 3222ft	Ciste Dhubh .... keesta doo	Black Chest......................	062166
❑ 981m 3218ft	Maol Chinn Dearg............ moul cheen jer-ak	Bald Red Head..................	032088
❑ 974m 3195ft	Beinn Sgritheall .... bay-n [ben] skree-tyal	Gravel Mountain...............	836126

Height	Mountain	Translation	Map Ref.
960m 3148ft	**Stob a'Choire Odhair** .... stop a chora [korry] oh-er	Peak of the Speckled Hollow	
❑ **959m** 3146ft	**Saileag** .... saal-ayk	Notched Heel	018148
❑ **953m** 3127ft	**Sgurr nan Coireachan** ...... skoor nan cor-ach-an	Peak of the Hollows	933958
❑ **947m** 3107ft	**Creag a'Mhaim** .... kray-k a veem	Rock of Horror	088078
❑ **946m** 3103ft	**Meall Buidhe** .... me-yal boo-ya [boo-ee]	Yellow Hill	849989
❑ **945m** 3100ft	**Sgurr na Sgine** .... skoor na skee-na	Peak of the Knife	946113
940m 3083ft	**Spidean Dhomhuill Bhric** speet-yan do-ool vrik	Peak of Spotted Donald	
❑ **939m** 3080ft	**Luinne Bheinn** .... loon-na vay-n [ven]	Angry Mountain...............	868008
929m 3047ft	**Sgurr nan Saighead** .... skoor nan say-yat	Peak of the Arrows	
❑ **920m** 3018ft	**An Socach** .... an soch-ach	The Beak...........................	088230
920m 3018ft	**Bealach Coire Ghaidheil** . b-yal-ach cora [korry] chal	The Pass of the Hollow of the Gaels	
919m 3015ft	**Sgurr Leac nan Each** .... skoor l-yech-t [lech-t] nan yach	Peak of the Slab of the Horse	
❑ **919m** 3015ft	**Gairich** .... ga-reech	Mountain of Laughter.......	025995
❑ **918m** 3012ft	**Creag nan Damh**............. kray-k nan dav	Rock of the Stags	983112
❑ **918m** 3012ft	**A'Ghlas Bheinn**................ a chlas vay-n [ven]	The Green Mountain.........	008231
○ **913m** 2995ft	**Sgurr a'Choire Bheithe**.... skoor a cora [korry] bee	Peak of the Birch Hollow ..	895015
906m 2972ft	**Sgurr Thionail**.................. skoor tee-on-al	Peak of the Gathering	
○ **901m** 2956ft	**Sgurr an Fhuarain**........... skoor an foor-an	Peak of the Well	987980
896m 2939ft	**Sgurr Beag**...................... skoor bay-k [beg]	Little Peak	
○ **894m** 2933ft	**Sgurr nan Eugallt**............ skoor nan eg-alt	Peak of the Dead Stream ..	931045
890m 2919ft	**Sgurr Beag**...................... skoor bay-k [beg]	Little Peak	
○ **887m** 2910ft	**Ben Aden** .... ben aa-ten	Hill of the Face.................	899986
○ **885m** 2903ft	**Sgurr a'Bhac Chaolais**..... skoor a vach choul-ash	Peak of the Hollow .... of the Narrows	958110

Height	Mountain	Translation	Map Ref.
881m 2890ft	**Sgurr Sgiath Airigh**.......... skoor skee-ah arry	Peak of the Winged Pasture	
○ **880m** 2887ft	**Sgurr Mhurlagain** .... skoor voo-la-kan	Peak of the Bay-shaped .. Sea-Inlet	012944
879m 2883ft	**Buidhe Bheinn** .... boo-ya vay-n [boo-ee ven]	Yellow Hill	
876m 2873ft	**Sgurr na Moraich**........... skoor na more-ach	Peak of Dignity	
873m 2863ft	**An Eag**............................ an ayk	The Notch	
○ **867m** 2844ft	**Sgurr na h-Aide** .... skoor na heej	Peak of the Hat.................	889931
○ **858m** 2815ft	**Fraoch Bheinn** .... frou-ch vay-n [ven]	Heather Hill......................	986940
856m 2808ft	**Creag Ghlas**..................... kray-k chlas	Green Rock	
○ **855m** 2805ft	**Beinn Bhuidhe** .... bay-n voo-ya [ben voo-ee]	Yellow Hill	822967
849m 2785ft	**Stob a'Chearcail**............. stop a cheer-kal	Circular Peak	
○ **841m** 2759ft	**Sgurr an Airgoid** .... skoor an er-e-kit	Peak of Silver	940227
○ **838m** 2749	**Sgurr Gaorsaic**................. skoor gour-sak	Peak of Horror..................	036218
○ **835m** 2739ft	**Sgurr Cos na Breachd**...... **Laoigh** skoor kos na brechk [breck]	Peak of the Cave of the..... Speckled Calf lou-ch	948947
○ **829m** 2720ft	**Carn Mor**........................ karn more	Big Hill.............................	903910
815m 2673ft	**Druim a'Chuirn** .... droom [drim] a choorn	Ridge of the Cairn	
○ **804m** 2638ft	**Beinn na h-Eaglaise** .... bay-n [ben] heg-lish	Hill of the Church	854120
○ **798m** 2618ft	**Am Bathach** .... am ba-tach	The Byre	073144
○ **796m** 2611ft	**Sgurr Coire Choinnichean** skoor cora [korry] chon-yeech-an	Peak of the Mossy Hollow	791011
○ **790m** 2591ft	**Druim na Cnamh**............... droom [drim] na krav	Ridge of the Chewing	131077
○ **785m** 2575ft	**Beinn na Caillich** .... bay-n [ben] na kal-yeech	Old Woman's Hill..............	796067
○ **781m** 2562ft	**Sgurr Mhic Bharraich** ...... skoor vic var-rach	Peak of the Son of Maurice	917174
776m 2545ft	**Sgurr Airigh na Beinne**.... skoor arry na bay-na	Peak of the Hill Pasture	

Height	Mountain	Translation	Map Ref.
○ 773m	**Beinn nan Caorach**	Hill of the Sheep	871122
2536ft	bayn [ben] nan kou-rach		
747m	**Sgurr na Meirleach**	Peak of the Thief	
2450ft	skoor na merl-yach		
742m	**Beinn a'Chapuill**	Hill of the Horse	
2434ft	bay-n [ben] a cha-fool		
740m	**Meall a'Choire Dhuibh**	Hill of the Black Hollow	
2427ft	me-yal a cora [korry] doo		
739m	**Sgurr Dubh**	Black Peak	
2424ft	skoor doo		
728m	**Sgurr Breac**	Speckled Hill	
2388ft	skoor brechk [breck]		
713m	**Druim Fada**	Long Ridge	
2339ft	droom [drim] fata		
709m	**Sgurr na Laire Brice** :........	Peak of the Piebald Mare	
2326ft	skoor na la-ra breeka		
702m	**Beinn Bhuidhe**	Yellow Hill	
2303ft	bay-n voo-ya [ben voo-ee]		
686m	**Meall Coire an t-Searaich**	Hill of the Hollow of the Foal	
2250ft	me-yal cora [korry] an t-yeer-ach		
666m	**Meall nan Eun**	Hill of the Birds	
2184ft	me-yal nan ayn		
656m	**Meall Blair**	Hill Clearing	
2152ft	me-yal blay-r		
631m	**Boc Mor**	Big male-goat	
2070ft	bok more		
627m	**Sgurr Mor**	Big Peak	
2057ft	skoor more		
616m	**Beinn Clachach**	Stony Hill	
2020ft	bayn [ben] klach-ach		
612m	**Sgurr Mor**	Big Peak	
2007ft	skoor more		
610m	**Ben Aslak**	Hill of the River Hollow	
2000ft	ben as-lak		

SKYE

739m	**Sgurr na Coinnich**	Peak of the Moss	
2424ft	skoor na chon-yeech		
733m	**Beinn nan Callich**	Hill of the Old Woman	
2404ft	bay-n [ben] nan kal-yeech		

34 *Fort Augustus and Glen Shiel*
(12 Munros)
(15 Corbetts)

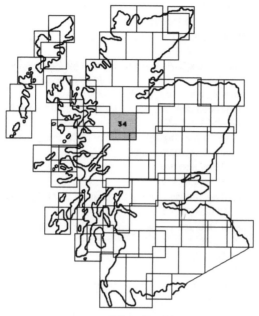

© Crown Copyright

34 FORT AUGUSTUS AND GLEN SHIEL

Height	Mountain	Translation	Map Ref.
❏ **1130m** 3707ft	**Creag Meagaidh** kray-k meg-ay	Bogland Rock	418875
❏ **1120m** 3674ft	**A'Chralaig** a chral-ak	The Basket	094148
❏ **1110m** 3642ft	**Sgurr nan Conbhairrean** skoor nan kon-a-vay-ran	Peak of the Hound Keeper	130139
❏ **1102m** 3615ft	**Mullach Fraoch Choire** mool-lach frou-ch chora [korry]	Summit of the Heather Hollow	095171
❏ **1053m** 3454ft	**Stob Poite Coire Ardair** stop poy-t cora [korry] ar-tir	Peak of the Pot of the High Hollow	429889
1052m 3451ft	**Beinn a'Chaorainn** bay-n [ben] a chou-ran	Mountain of the Rowan Tree	386851
1027m 3369ft	**Meall Choire Choille-Rais** me-yal chora choola [korry kolly] rash	Hill of the Wooded Hollow	

Height	Mountain	Translation	Map Ref.
❏ 1006m 3300ft	**Carn Liath** .... karn lee-ah	Grey Mountain.................	472903
❏ 1002m 3287ft	**Sail Chaorainn**................. saal chou-ran	Heel of the Rowan Tree	133155
1001m 3283ft	**Sron a' Choire**.................. srawn a chora [korry]	Point of the Hollow	
993m 3257ft	**An Cearcallach** .... an k-yar-kal-ach	The Hoop	
991m 3250ft	**Sron Coire a'Chriochairein** srawn a cora [korry] a chree-och-ar-in	Point of the Hollow of the. Boundary Keeper	
❏ 957m 3140ft	**Carn Ghluasaid**................ karn chloo-ash-at	Mountain of Movement	146125
❏ 935m 3067ft	**Sron a'Choire Ghairbh**..... srawn a chora [korry] charv	Point of the Rough Hollow	222945
929m 3047ft	**Tigh Mor na Seilge**.......... ti more na sheel-ka	Big House of the Hunt	
❏ 917m 3008ft	**Meall na Teanga** .... me-yal na t-yen-ga	Mountain of the Tongue ...	220925
❏ 915m 3002ft	**Beinn Teallach**................. bay-n [ben] t-yeel-lach	Hill of the Hearth	361860
◯ 901m 2955ft	**Ben Tee**........................... ben t-yee	Fairy Hill	241972
◯ 896m 2939ft	**Corrieyairack** .... korry-yer-ack	Hill of the Rising Glen.......	429998
◯ 896m 2939ft	**Gairbeinn**....................... gar-bay-n [ben]	Rough Hill	460985
892m 2926ft	**Meall a Chaorainn Mor** ... me-yal a chou-ran more	Big Hill of the Rowan Tree	
◯ 889m 2916ft	**Aonach Shasuinn**............ ou-nach [an-ach] saa-sin	Englishman's Ridge..........	173180
888m 2913ft	**Carn Dearg**....................... karn jer-ak	Red Hill	
887m 2910ft	**Sean Mheall** .... shen ve-yal	Stormy Hill	
884m 2890ft	**Carn Leac**........................ karn l-ye-cht [le-cht]	Slab Hill	
876m 2873ft	**Geal Charn**....................... g-yal charn	White Hill	
◯ 863m 2830ft	**Carn a Choire Chairbh**..... karn a chora [korry] char-av	Hill of the Hollow.............. of the Carcass	137189
859m 2818ft	**Sron a'Bhuirich**................ srawn a voo-reech	Point of the Bellowing	
849m 2785ft	**Creag a'Bhanain**.............. kray-k a van-in	White Rocks	

Height	Mountain	Translation	Map Ref.
845m 2772ft	**An Reithe** an ree-ah	The Ram	
○ **838m** 2749ft	**Meall na h-Eilde** me-yal na heel-j	Hill of the Deer	185946
837m 2745ft	**Meall Dubh** me-yal doo	Black Hill	
○ **834m** 2736ft	**Carn Dearg** karn jer-ak	Red Hill	345887
833m 2733ft	**Bac Nam Fuaran** bak nam foor-an	Bank of the Spring	
817m 2680ft	**Meall a'Mheanbh-chroidh** me-yal a ven-av-chro	Hill of the Small Cattle	
817m 2680m	**Beannain Beaga** ben-nan bay-ka	Small Hills	
○ **816m** 2677ft	**Carn a'Chuilinn** karn a chool-inn	Holly Hill	416034
815m 2674ft	**Meall Ptarmigan** m-yal tar-mi-kan	Ptarmigan Hill	
○ **815m** 2674ft	**Carn Dearg** karn jer-ak	Red Hill	349967
○ **804m** 2637ft	**Geal Charn** g-yal charn	White Hill	156943
○ **800m** 2625ft	**Beinn Iaruinn** bay-n [ben] ear-oon	Iron Hill	296900
○ **796m** 2611ft	**Beinn Bhan** bay-n [ben] van	White Hill	141857
○ **790m** 2591ft	**Druim na Cnamh** droom [drim] na krav	Ridge of the Chewing	131077
789m 2588ft	**Coire Beithe** cora [korry] bee	Birch Hollow	
○ **788m** 2585ft	**Meall Dubh** me-yal doo	Black Hill	245078
779m 2555ft	**An Doire** an dor-ee [dora]	The Thicket	
778m 2552ft	**Carn Easgann Bana** karn es-kan bana	Hill of the White Eel	
775m 2542ft	**Beinn Loinne** bay-n [ben] loy-na	Hill of the Glade	
771m 2529ft	**Beinn Bhan** bay-n [ben] van	White Hill	
○ **768m** 2520ft	**Carn Dearg** karn jer-ak	Red Hill	357948
764m 2506ft	**Creag Mhor** kray-k voar	Big Rock	
761m 2496ft	**Meall an Tagraidh** me-yal an tak-ray	Hill of the Pleading	

Height	Mountain	Translation
761m 2496ft	**Meall Caca**.................... me-yal kach	Dirty Hill
760m 2493ft	**Creag Chail**..................... kray-k cheel	Hill of the Husk
749m 2457ft	**Sgurr Choinnich**.............. skoor chon-yeech	Peak of the Moss
746m 2447ft	**Binnein Shuas** .... bin-yan soo-as	Upward Pinnacle
745m 2444ft	**Carn na Larach** .... karn na lar-ach	Hill of the Ruin
736m 2414ft	**Carn Dearg**...................... karn jer-ak	Red Hill
732m 2401ft	**Glas Bheinn** .... glas vay-n [ven]	Green Hill
732m 2401ft	**Carn nam Feuaich** .... karn nam fee-yach	Angry Hill
723m 2371ft	**Carn Bhrunachain**........... karn vroon-ach-an	Hill of the Rumbling
722m 2368ft	**Cnap na Stri**.................... krap na stree	Lump of Strife
719m 2359ft	**Creag Tharsuinn** .... kray-k tar-sinn	Transverse Hill
715m 2345ft	**Creag Mhaigh** .... kray-k vay	May Hill
714m 2442ft	**Mam Chroisg** .... mam chrosh-k	Cross Hill
704m 2309ft	**Carn a'Chaochain** .... karn a chou-chan	Hill of the Streamlet
704m 2309ft	**Creag Coire Doe** .... kray-k cora [korry] doo	Hill of the Black Hollow
700m 2296ft	**Meall nan Aighean Mor**... me-yal nan ay-yan more	Big Hill of the Hinds
696m 2283ft	**Meall Fuar-Mhonaidh**...... me-yal foor von-ay	Hill of the Cold Moor
695m 2280ft	**Leana Mor** .... lee-ana more	Big Meadow
689m 2260ft	**Meall na Dearcag**............ me-yal na jer-kag	Hill of the Little Berries
680m 2230ft	**Carn Mhic an Toisich**....... karn vic an tosh-eech	Macintosh Hill
678m 2224ft	**Leana Mhor** .... lee-ana voar	Big Meadow
674m 2211ft	**Clach Criche** .... klach kreech	Boundary Rock
663m 2175ft	**Carn nan Earb**................. karn nan erb	Hill of Roe Deer

Height	Mountain	Translation
660m 2165ft	**Beinn an Eoin** .... bay-n [ben] an yawn	Hill of the Bird
660m 2165ft	**Meall Tarsuinn** .... me-yal tar-sinn	Transverse Hill
658m 2159ft	**Creag Dhubh** .... kray-k doo	Black Rock
654m 2145ft	**Coire Ceirsle** .... cora [korry] keer-sla	Hill of the Clew
648m 2125ft	**Glas Bheinn** .... glas vay-n [ven]	Green Hill
648m 2125ft	**Carn a'Choire Leith** .... karn a cora [korry] lay	Hill of the Half Hollow
645m 2116ft	**Ruighe na Beinne** .... roo-ya na bay-na	Base of the Hill
641m 2102ft	**Teanga Bheag** .... t-yen-ka vay-k [beg]	Little Tongue
635m 2083ft	**Creag Liath** .... kray-k lee-ah	Grey Hill
623m 2043ft	**Na Cnapanan** .... na krap-an-an	The Lumps
616m 2020ft	**Beinn Chraoibh** .... bayn [ben] chrouv	Tree Hill
611m 2004ft	**Meallan Odhar** .... me-yal-an oh-er	Dappled Hill

35 Kingussie and Monadhliath

(5 Munros)
(5 Corbetts)

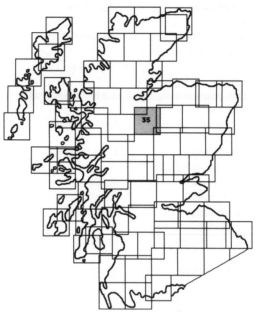

© Crown Copyright

35 KINGUSSIE AND MONADHLIATH

Height	Mountain	Translation	Map Ref.
1052m 3451ft	**Carn Ban Mor** karn ban more	Big White Hill	
❑ **1019m** 3342ft	**Mullach Clach a'Bhlair** mool-lach klach av-lar	Summit of the Stony Plain´	883927
998m 3273ft	**Meall Dubhag** me-yal doo-ak	Hill of the Black One	
976m 3201ft	**Meall Tional** me-yal tee-nal	Gathering Hill	
❑ **945m** 3100ft	**Carn Dearg** karn jer-ak	Red Mountain	635024
942m 3090ft	**Carn Ban** karn ban	White Hill	
❑ **930m** 3051ft	**A'Chailleach** a chal-yach	The Old Woman	681041
❑ **926m** 3038ft	**Geal Charn** g-yal charn	White Mountain	561988

Height	Mountain	Translation	Map Ref.
❑ 920m 3018ft	**Carn Sgulain**................... karn skoo-lan	Mountain of the Basket ...	684059
920m 3018ft	**Geal Charn**...................... g-yal charn	White Hill	
918m 3011ft	**Druim nan Bo**.................. droom [drim] nan boo	Ridge of the Cows	
909m 2982ft	**Meall a'Bhothain**............. me-yal a vo-han	Hill of the Hut	
897m 2942ft	**Carn Odhar na Criche** ...... karn oh-er na kreech	Hill of the Dappled Boundary	
891m 2922ft	**Geal Charn**...................... g-yal charn	White Hill	
887m 2909ft	**Beinn Sgiath** .... bay-n [ben] skee-ah	Hill of the Wing	
◯ 878m 2880ft	**Carn an Fhreiceadain**...... karn an free-ka-tan	Hill of the Watchers..........	726071
873m 2864ft	**Carn Donnachaidh Beag**.. karn don-ach-ay bay-k [beg]	Small Hill of the Robertsons	
◯ 862m 2828ft	**Meall na h-Airse**............. me-yal na heer-sha	Hill of the Defile...............	515000
862m 2828ft	**Carn na Criche**................. karn na kreech	Hill of the Boundary	
858m 2814ft	**Sgaraman nan Fiadh**....... skar-man nan fee-ay	Joints of the Deer	
844m 2768ft	**Leathad Gaothach** .... lay-hat gou-tach	Windy Slope	
843m 2765ft	**Carn an Liath** .... karn an lee-ah	Grey Hill	
834m 2736ft	**Marg na Craige**................ merk na kray-ka	Silver Coin Rock	
828m 2716ft	**Burrach Mor**..................... boor-rach more	Big Digging	
826m 2709ft	**Carn Coire na Creiche** ..... karn cora [korry] na kreech	Hill of the Hollow Boundary	
◯ 824m 2703ft	**Geal Charn Mor** .... g-yal charn more	Big White Hill....................	837124
814m 2670ft	**Calpa Mor** .... kalpa more	Big Nail	
812m 2663ft	**Carn Sgulain**................... karn skoo-lan	Hill of the Basket	
◯ 811m 2661ft	**Carn na Saobhaide**.......... karn na sou-vay	Hill of the Fox's Den	600145
809m 2654ft	**Carn na Laraiche Maoile**. karn na lar-ach moula	Hill of the Bare Ruin	
808m 2651ft	**Carn Icean Duibhe**........... karn Iken doo	Black Hill	

Height	Mountain	Translation	Map Ref.
807m 2648ft	**Beinn Bhreac Mor**............ ban vrechk more [ben vreck more]	Big Speckled Hill	
805m 2640ft	**Carn Ghriogar**................. karn chree-kar	MacGregor's Hill	
802m 2631ft	**Carn Odhar**...................... karn oh-er	Dappled Hill	
800m 2624ft	**Coire Garbhlach**.............. cora [korry] garv-lach	Rough Hollow	
795m 2608ft	**Meallan Dubh** .... me-yal-lan doo	Black Hill	
791m 2594ft	**Carn a'Choire Sheilich** .... karn a chora [korry] sheel-eech	Hill of the Willow Tree Hollow	
790m 2591ft	**Carn Coire na h-Eagsgain** karn cora [korry] na hay-skan	Hill of the Hollow of the Eel	
789m 2587ft	**Carn Dearg**...................... karn jer-ak	Red Hill	
787m 2580ft	**Doire Meurach**................. dor-ee [dora] mer-ach	Knotty Thicket	
786m 2577ft	**Creag Dubh**..................... kray-k doo	Black Rock	
780m 2559ft	**Beinn Bhuraich** .... bay-n [ben] voo-rach	Digging Hill	
778m 2552ft	**Carn a'Choire Ghlaise** ..... karn a chora [korry] chlasha	Hill of the Green Hollow	
774m 2539ft	**Ileach Bhan**..................... eel-yach van	White Islayman	
771m 2529ft	**Meallan Odhar**................. me-yal oh-er	Dappled Hill	
○ **769m** 2522ft	**Meallach Mhor** .... me-yal-lach voar	Big Hill	777909
767m 2516ft	**Carn Dubh**....................... karn doo	Black Hill	
765m 2509ft	**Carn Fraoich** .... karn frou-ch	Heather Hill	
758m 2486ft	**An Sguabach**................... an skoo-pach	The Brush	
757m 2484ft	**Creag Dubh**..................... kray-k doo	Black Hill	
756m 2480ft	**Sidhean Dubh na Cloiche Baine** shee-yan doo na kloy-ch ban-ya	Black Fairy Hillock of the White Stone	
750m 2460ft	**Carn Dubh Ican Deoir**...... karn doo Iken jee-or	Black Hill of the Tears	
746m 2447ft	**Carn Coire Easgrabath** .... karn cora [korry] es-kra-ta	Hill of the Waterfall Hollows	

Height	Mountain	Translation
745m 2444ft	**Cnoc Fraing** .... krok frenk	French Hillock
745m 2444ft	**Creag Liath** .... kray-k lee-ah	Grey Rock
741m 2430ft	**Geal Charn Beag**............. g-yal charn bay-k [beg]	Small White Hill
729m 2391ft	**A'Bhuidheanaich** .... a voo-yan-ach	The Quarry
726m 2381ft	**Carn Luibean Glas**........... karn loob-yan glas	Hill of the Grey Weeds
725m 2378ft	**Carn Gearresith** .... karn g-yar-shee	Hill of the Darting Hare
722m 2368ft	**Carn Dubh**....................... karn doo	Black Hill
716m 2345ft	**Carn Ban Beag**................. karn ban bay-k [beg]	Small White Hill
712m 2335ft	**Creag na Cailleach**.......... kray-k na kal-yach	Old Woman's Rock
712m 2335ft	**Carn Dearg Mor** .... karn jer-ak more	Big Red Hill
711m 2332ft	**Beinn Bhuidhe** .... bay-n voo-ya [ben voo-ee]	Yellow Hill
707m 2319ft	**Carn Liath Bhaid**.............. karn lee-ah vat	Hill of the Grey Clothing
700m 2296ft	**Meall nan Ruadhag**......... me-yal na roo-yak	Hill of the Young Roe Deer
699m 2293ft	**Carn Airighe na Eag**......... karn arry na ayk	Hill of the Notched Pasture
694m 2276ft	**Carn Dearg Beag** .... karn jer-ak bay-k [beg]	Small Red Hill
689m 2260ft	**Beinn Dubhchraidh**.......... bay-n [ben] doo-chray	Hill of Black Piety
684m 2244ft	**Carn Coire Dhealanaich** .. karn cora [korry] yal-an-eech	Hill of the Lightning Hollow
682m 2237ft	**Beinn Acha Bhraghad**...... bay-n [ben] ach vra-chat	Hill of the Upper Field
679m 2227ft	**Carn Sleamhainn**............. karn shlee-van	Slippery Hill
675m 2214ft	**Coille Mhor**...................... kool-a [kolly] voar	Big Woodland
674m 2211ft	**Carn an Rathaid Dhuibh** .. karn an rah-at doo	Hill of the Black Roadway
663m 2175ft	**Carn Odhar**....................... karn oh-er	Dappled Hill
658m 2158ft	**Meall a'Bhuailt**................ me-yal a voo-alt	Hill of Quarrel

Height	Mountain	Translation
656m 2152ft	**Carn Fliuch-Bhaid**............ karn flooch-vat	Hill of Wet Clothing
652m 2139ft	**Meall a'Ghiubhais**........... me-yal a choo-vash	Hill of the Pine Trees
650m 2132ft	**Carn Leachtar Dubh**......... karn lech-tar doo	Big Fairy Hill
650m 2132ft	**Sith Mor**........................... shee more	Big Peace
648m 2125ft	**Carn Bad an Daimh** .... karn bad an dav	Hill of the Deer Cluster
642m 2106ft	**Aonach Odhar**.................. ou-nach [an-ach] oh-er	Dappled Ridge
636m 2086ft	**Carn Coire na Caorach** .... karn cora [korry] na kou-rach	Hill of the Hollow of the Sheep
634m 2080ft	**Carn na Bain Tighearna**... karn na ban ti-yar-na	Hill of the Countess
634m 2080ft	**Carn Loisge** .... karn losh-k	Fiery Hill
632m 2074ft	**Carn Doire na h-Achlais** .. karn dor-ee [dora] na ach-lash	Hill of the Thicket Hollow
631m 2070ft	**Carn Glac an Eich** .... karn glak an ech	Hill of the Horse's Hollow
631m 2070ft	**Carn Coire Dhugain** .... karn cora [korry] doo-kan	Hill of the Hollow of Black Sand
627m 2057ft	**Carn an Uillt Tharsuinn** ... karn an oolt tar-sinn	Hill of the Transverse Stream
627m 2057ft	**Carn a'Choire Mhoir** .... karn a cora [korry] voar	Hill of the Big Hollow
626m 2054ft	**Clach Mheall** .... klach ve-yal	Stone Hill
622m 2041ft	**Sguman Mor** .... skoo-man more	Big Boat Bailing Dish
619m 2031ft	**Clach Mheall Dubh** .... klach ve-yal doo	Black Stone Hill
618m 2027ft	**Carn Phris Maoir** .... karn preesh mour	Hill of the Esteemed Officer

36 Grantown, Aviemore and Cairngorm
(15 Munros)
(8 Corbetts)

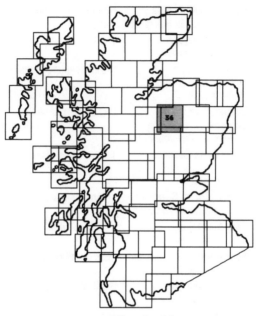

© Crown Copyright

36 GRANTOWN, AVIEMORE AND CAIRNGORM

Height	Mountain	Translation	Map Ref.
☐ **1309m** 4295ft	**Ben MacDui** .... ben mak-doo-i	Mountain of the Son of Duff	989989
☐ **1296m** 4252ft	**Braeriach** .... bray-reech	Upper Part........................	953999
☐ **1293m** 4242ft	**Cairn Toul** .... karn [kayr-n] tool	Hill of the Barn	963972
1258m 4126ft	**Sgor an Lochan Uaine** ..... skoor an loch-an oo-ayn	Peak of the Little Green Loch	
☐ **1245m** 4085ft	**Cairn Gorm** .... karn gor-om [kayr-n gor-m]	Blue Mountain	005041
1215m 3985ft	**Cairn Lochan** .... karn [kayr-n] loch-an	Hill of the Little Loch	
1213m 3976ft	**Stob Coire an Saighdeir** .. stop cora [korry] an say-jir	Peak of the Hollow of the Soldier	

Height	Mountain	Translation	Map Ref.
❏ 1196m 3924ft	**Beinn a'Bhuird**.................. bay-n [ben] a voort	Table Mountain.................	093006
1184m 3883ft	**Sron na Lairge**................... srawn na la-rig	Point of the Pass	
❏ 1182m 3878ft	**Beinn Mheadhoin**............ bay-n [ben] vee-yon	Middle Mountain	024017
1176m 3857ft	**Coire an t'Sneachda**........ cora an trech-ta [korry an sh-nech-ta]	Hollow of the Snow	
1172m 3844ft	**Cnap a' Chleirich**............. krap a chler-eech	The Clergyman's Lump	
	Ben Avon........................... ben an Highest peak:	River Mountain (possible translation)	
❏ 1171m 3841ft	**Leabaidh an Daimh** .... **Bhuidhe** l-ye-pay an dav voo-ya [voo-ee]	Bed of the Yellow Stag	132019
❏ 1155m 3789ft	**Derry Cairn Gorm** .... derry karn gor-om [kayr-n gor-m]	Thicket of the Blue .... Mountain	017980
1151m 3775ft	**Cnap Coire na'Spreidhe** .. krap cora [korry] na spray	Lumpy Hollow of the Cattle	
1120m 3673ft	**Carn Etchachan**................ karn et-shach-an	Hill of the Fired Heather	
❏ 1118m 3667ft	**Sgor Gaoithe**...................... skoor gou-ee	Peak of the Wind	903989
1111m 3644ft	**Sgoran Dubh Mor** .... skoor-an doo more	Big Black Peak	
1110m 3640ft	**Sron Riach** .... srawn ree-ach	Grey Point	
1108m 3635ft	**Creagan a'Choire**............. krayk-an a chora [korry]	Rocky Hollow	
1106m 3629ft	**Stob an t'Sluichd** .... stop an t-looch-t [sloocht]	Pillar of the Swallowing	
❏ 1090m 3576ft	**Bynack Mhor**...................... ben-ak voar	Big Hill of the Cap	042063
1089m 3572ft	**Carn Eas**........................... karn es	Waterfall Hill	
❏ 1082m 3550ft	**Beinn a Chaorainn**........... bay-n [ben] a chou-ran	Mountain of the .... Rowan Tree	045013
1082m 3550ft	**Stob Coire Etchachan** ...... stop cora [korry] et-shach-an	Peak of the Hollow of the Fired Heather	
1076m 3529ft	**Stob Bac an Fhurain** .... stop bak an foor-an	Peak of the Bank of the Well	
1053m 3454ft	**Creag an Leith-Choin** ...... kray-k an lay choy-n	Rock of the Half Dog	

Height	Mountain	Translation	Map Ref.
1052m 3451ft	**Carn Ban Mor**................... karn ban more	Big White Hill	
❏ **1037m** 3401ft	**Carn a'Mhaim**.................. karn a vay-m	Rounded Mountain..........	994952
❏ **1019m** 3342ft	**Mullach a Clach a'Bhlair**. mool-ach a klach av-lar	Summit of the Stony Plain	883927
1017m 3336ft	**A'Choinneach** .... a chon-yach	The Moss	
1015m 3329ft	**Beinn a Choarainn Beag**.. bayn a chou-ran bay-k [beg]	Hill of the Little Rowan Tree	
❏ **1004m** 3293ft	**The Devil's Point**.............	....	976951
983m 3224ft	**Sgurr an Lochan Uaine**.... skoor an loch-an oo-ayn	Peak of the Little Green Loch	
972m 3188ft	**Creag an Dail Mhor** .... kray-kan dal voar	Big Rock of the River Meadow	
❏ **931m** 3054ft	**Beinn Bhreac** .... bayn vrechk [ben vreck]	Speckled Mountain...........	058971
930m 3050ft	**Big Brae**........................... big bray	Big Slope	
920m 3018ft	**Geal Carn**......................... g-yal karn	White Hill	
918m 3011ft	**Tom Dubh** .... toam [tom] doo	Black Mound	
911m 2988ft	**Meall Gaineimh**............... me-yal gan-eev	Sandy Hill	
⃝ **900m** 2953ft	**Culdaroch** .... kool-dar-och	Back High Place................	193988
895m 2936ft	**Carn Crom**....................... karn krom	Rounded Hill	
⃝ **895m** 2936ft	**Creag Mhor** .... kray-k voar	Big Rock............................	057048
⃝ **862m** 2828ft	**Carn Liath** .... karn lee-ah	Grey Hill	165977
862m 2828ft	**Creag an Dail Bheag** .... kray-k an dal vay-k [beg]	Little Rock of the River Meadow	
848m 2781ft	**Creag Dhubh**.................... kray-k doo	Black Rock	
⃝ **829m** 2720ft	**Brown Cow Hill**...............	....	221044
⃝ **821m** 2694m	**Geal Charn**....................... g-yal charn	White Hill...........................	090127
⃝ **818m** 2683ft	**Carn na Drochaide**........... karn na droch-at	Hill of the Bridge..............	127938
⃝ **810m** 2657ft	**Meall a Bhuachaille** .... me-yal a vooch-al	Herdsman Hill...................	991115

99

Height	Mountain	Translation	Map Ref.
807m 2647ft	**Carn Fiaclach** karn fee-klach	Toothed Hill	
802m 2631ft	**Meikle Geal Charn** me-kil g-yal charn	Big White Hill	
799m 2621ft	**Meall Tional** me-yal tee-on-al	Hill of Gathering	
○ 792m 2598ft	**Carn Ealasaid** karn yala-sat	Elizabeth's Hill	228118
787m 2581m	**Creag a'Chalamain** kray-k a chal-a-man	Rock of Doves	
784m 2572ft	**Carn Eag Dhubh** karn ayk doo	Black Notch Hill	
776m 2545ft	**Beinn a Chruinnich** bay-n [ben] a chroon-eech	Gathering Hill	
772m 2532ft	**Carn Dearg** karn jer-ak	Red Hill	
759m 2490ft	**Geal Charn Beag** g-yal charn bay-k [beg]	Small White Hill	
759m 2490ft	**Carn Tarsuinn** karn tar-sinn	Transverse Hill	
743m 2437ft	**Carn Drochaid** karn droch-at	Hill of the Bridge	
742m 2434ft	**Carn Eilrig** karn eel-rik	Deer Trap Hill	
742m 2434ft	**Stac na h-Iolaire** stak na h-yool-ir	Stack of the Eagle	
741m 2441ft	**Big Garvoun** big garv-oon	Big Rough One	
739m 2424ft	**Carn na Criche** karn na kreech	Hill of the Boundary	
735m 2411ft	**Monadhanan Eun** mona-yan ayn	Moorland of the Bird	
734m 2408ft	**Carn Odhar** karn oh-er	Dappled Hill	
733m 2405ft	**Meall an t-Slugain** me-yal an t-loo-kan [sloo-kan]	Hill of the Swallowing	
732m 2401ft	**Creagan Gorm** kray-kan gor-om	Blue Rocks	
730m 2395ft	**Carn na Feannaige** karn na f-yan-na-ka	Hill of the Hooded Crow	
728m 2388ft	**Bile Buidhe** beel boo-ya [boo-ee]	Great Yellow Tree	
726m 2381ft	**Carn na Craoibhe** karn na krouv	Hill of the Tree	
722m 2368ft	**Creag a'Chaise** kray-k a chash	Steep Rock	

Height	Mountain	Translation
721m 2365ft	**Little Garvoun** .... little garv-oon	Little Rough One
716m 2348ft	**Carn Ban Beag** .... karn ban bay-k [beg]	Little White Hill
714m 2342ft	**Cnap Chaochan Aitinn** ..... krap chou-chan ay-tin	Lump of the Juniper Stream
714m 2342ft	**The Bruach** .... the broo-ach	The Bank
710m 2329ft	**Carn a Ghille Chearr** .... karn a gilly ch-yar	Hill of the Wronged Boy
710m 2329ft	**Little Geal Charn** .... little g-yal charn	Little White Hill
709m 2326ft	**Meikle Elrick** .... me-kil el-rik	Big Deer Trap
704m 2309ft	**Carn Oirghreag** .... karn oy-rak	Hill of the Cloud Berries
696m 2282ft	**Tom Bhreac** .... toam vrechk [tom breck]	Speckled Hill
694m 2276ft	**Cnap an Dobhrain** .... krap an dov-ran	Lump of the Otter
692m 2270ft	**Tolm Buirich** .... toll-m boor-eech	Hillock of the Bellowing
691m 2267ft	**Meall Glasail Mor** .... me-yal glash-al more	Big Greyish Hill
688m 2257ft	**Carn na Farraidh** .... karn na far-ray	Hill of the Company
686m 2250ft	**Cnapan a'Mheirlich** .... krap-an a veer-leech	Lump of Thieves
685m 2247ft	**Craig Gowrie** .... kray-k gow-ri	Goat Rock
664m 2178ft	**Liath Bheinn** .... lee-ah vay-n [ven]	Grey Hill
662m 2172ft	**Carn Clioche** .... karn kloy-ch	Stone Hill
650m 2132ft	**Creag a'Chleirich** .... kray-k a chler-eech	Hill of the Clergyman
649m 2129ft	**Creag a'Chait** .... kray-k a chat	Cat Rock
646m 2119ft	**Creag Tarmachain** .... kray-k tar-mach-an	Ptarmigan Rock
644m 2112ft	**Airgiod Meall** .... er-e-kit me-yal	Silver Hill
643m 2109ft	**Carn Moine** .... karn moy-n	Peat Hill
641m 2100ft	**Druim Loin** .... droom [drim] loy-n	Glade Ridge

Height	Mountain	Translation
638m 2092ft	**Carn Elrig Mor** .... karn el-rik more	Big Hill of the Deer Trap
634m 2079ft	**Carn Loisgie** .... karn losh-ka	Fiery Hill
633m 2076ft	**Carn Gruamach** .... karn groo-mach	Gloomy Hill
628m 2060ft	**Sgor Gaoithe** .... skoor gou-ee	Windy Hill
628m 2060ft	**Meall an t'Seangain** .... me-yal an t-yen-kan [shen-kan]	Hill of the Ants
622m 2040ft	**Creag nan Gall** .... kray-k nan gawl	Rock of the Lowlander
618m 2027ft	**Carn Ruadh Bhreac** .... karn roo-ah vrechk [vreck]	Speckled Red Hill
617m 2024ft	**Meall Gorm** .... me-yal gor-om	Blue Hill

37 Strathdon
(5 Corbetts)

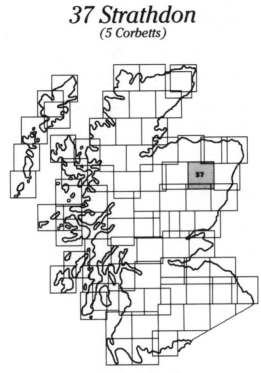

© Crown Copyright

37 STRATHDON

	Height	Mountain	Translation	Map Ref.
○	**871m** 2858ft	**Morven** more-ven	Big Hill	377040
○	**829m** 2720ft	**Brown Cow Hill**		221044
○	**804m** 2638ft	**Carn Mor** karn more	Big Hill	265183
	799m 2621ft	**Carn Liath** karn le-ah	Grey Hill	
	799m 2621ft	**Monadh an t-Stuichd Leith** mon-ah an toocht [stoo-cht] lay	Big Ridge of the Half Stack	
○	**792m** 2598ft	**Carn Ealasaid** karn yala-sat	Elizabeth's Hill	228118
	787m 2581ft	**Letterach** le-ter-ach	Big Hillside	
○	**781m** 2562ft	**Corryhabbie** korry-ha-bi	Pointed Hollow	281289

Height	Mountain	Translation
755m 2476ft	**Cook's Cairn**	
754m 2473ft	**Dun Mor** .... doon [dun] more	Big Fort
749m 2457ft	**Mona Gowan** .... mon-a gow-an	Goat Moor
744m 2440ft	**Carn Bhacain** .... karn vak-an	Peat Banks Hill
744m 2440ft	**Cairnagour** .... kayr-na-gour	Hill of the Goat
743m 2437ft	**Geallaig** .... g-yal-ig	White Hill
732m 2401ft	**Carn an t-Suidhe** .... karn an too-ya [soo-ya]	Hill of the Soot
731m 2398ft	**Carn na Glascoill** .... karn na glas-goy-l	Hill of the Grey Forest
729m 2391ft	**Muckle Lapprach** .... muck-il laf-rach	Big Hill of Weakness
718m 2355ft	**An Socach** .... an soch-ach	The Beak
683m 2240ft	**Geal Charn** .... g-yal charn	White Hill
673m 2207ft	**Geal Charn** .... g-yal charn	White Hill
655m 2148ft	**Carn Bhodaich** .... karn vo-tach	Old Man's Hill
651m 2135ft	**Carn Vachich** .... karn vach-eech	Peat Banks Hill
633m 2076ft	**Creag an Sgor** .... kray-k an skoor	Peak of the Rock
632m 2073ft	**Creag an Eunan** .... kra-y an ay-nan	Peak of the Bird
620m 2033ft	**Carn Allt a'Chlaiginn** .... karn all-t a chla-gin	Hill of the High Stream
607m 1991ft	**Corrienearn** .... cora-yarn	High Hollow
598m 1961ft	**Sron Aonghais** .... srawn an-gash	Angus's Point
594m 1949ft	**Carn Dearg** .... karn jer-ak	Red Hill
583m 1913ft	**Carn Odhar** .... karn oh-er	Dappled Hill
544m 1784ft	**Sgor an h-Iolaire** .... skoor an h-yool-ir	Peak of the Eagle
533m 1748ft	**Creagan Riabhach** .... kray-kan ree-vach	Grizzled Rocks

Height	Mountain	Translation
527m 1729ft	**Creag nan Ban**................. kray-kan nan ban	Rocks of the Women
489m 1604ft	**Cnoc Chalmac**................. krok chal-mak	Stout Hillock
486m 1594ft	**Creag Ghiubhais**.............. kray-k choo-vash	Rock of the Pine Tree
420m 1378ft	**Clachcurr** .... klach-coor	Stony Sowing Ground
411m 1348ft	**Tom Beith** .... toam [tom] bee	Mound of the Birch Tree

39 Rum and Eigg
(2 Corbetts)
46 Coll and Tiree

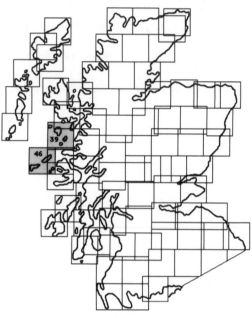

© Crown Copyright

39 RUM and EIGG

RUM

Height	Mountain	Translation	Map Ref.
○ **812m** 2664ft	**Askival** as-ki-val	Hill of the Ash Trees	393952
○ **781m** 2563ft	**Ainshval** ayn-sh-val	Hill of the Strong Hold	379944
764m 2506ft	**Sgurr nan Gillean** skoor nan geel-yan	Peak of the Young Men	
723m 2371ft	**Hallival** hal-li-val	unknown	
702m 2303ft	**Trallval** tral-val	unknown	
591m 1938ft	**Barkeval** bark-e-val	unknown	
571m 1873ft	**Oreval** or-e-val	Moor Fowl Hill	

Height	Mountain	Translation
556m 1824ft	**Ard Nev** .... ard neev	High Peak
546ft 1791ft	**Beinn nan Stac** .... bay-n [ben] nan stak	Hill of the Pillar
528m 1732ft	**Ruinsval** .... roo-ins-val	unknown
520m 1705ft	**Sron an t-Saighdeir** .... srawn an tay-jir [say-jir]	Point of the Soldier
463m 1519ft	**Fionchra** .... fee-on-chra	White Point
304m 914ft	**Mullach Mor** .... mool-lach more	Big Summit
263m 863ft	**An Dornbac** .... an dorn-bak	The Fists

EIGG

393m 1289ft	**An Sgurr** .... an skoor	The Peak
336m 1102ft	**Beinn Bhuidhe** .... bay-n boo-ya [ben boo-ee]	Yellow Hill
315m 1033ft	**Beinn Tighe** .... bay-n [ben] tee-ah	Thick Hill
299m 981ft	**An Cruachan** .... an kroo-ach-an	Rocky Stacks

CANNA

210m 689ft	**Carn a'Ghaill** .... karn a chal	Stormy Hill
149m 489ft	**Sliabh Mhedhonach** .... slee vee-yon-ach	Middle Hill of the Moor
139m 456ft	**Compass Hill**	

MUCK

137m 500ft	**Beinn Airein** .... bayn [ben] ayr-in	Plough Hill

46 COLL AND TIREE

No significant high ground.

40 Mallaig and North Shiel
(8 Munros)
(23 Corbetts)

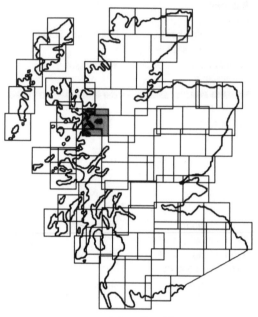

© Crown Copyright

40 MALLAIG AND NORTH SHIEL

	Height	Mountain	Translation	Map Ref.
❑	**1041m** 3415ft	**Sgurr na Ciche** .... skoor na keesh-ta	Peak of the Breast	902966
❑	**1013m** 3323ft	**Garbh Chioch Mhor** .... garv chee-och voar	Big Rough Place of the .... Breast	909961
❑	**1003m** 3290ft	**Sgurr Mor** .... skoor more	Big Peak	965980
❑	**987m** 3238ft	**Gaor Bheinn or Gulvain** ... gore vay-n [ven] or gool-van	Dirty Hill	003876
❑	**963m** 3159ft	**Sgur Thuilm** .... skoor hool-m	Peak of the Hillock............	939879
❑	**956m** 3136ft	**Sgurr nan Coireachan** ...... skoor nan kor-ach-an	Peak of the Hollows..........	903880
❑	**953m** 3127ft	**Sgurr nan Coireachan** ...... skoor nan kor-ach-an	Peak of the Hollows..........	933958
❑	**946m** 3104ft	**Meall Buidhe** .... me-yal boo-ya [boo-ee]	Yellow Mountain...............	849989

Height	Mountain	Translation	Map Ref.
○ 909m 2982ft	**The Streap** .... the streep	Climbing Hill....................	946863
○ 901m 2955ft	**Sgurr an Fhuarain**........... skoor an foor-an	Peak of the Well	987980
896m 2939ft	**Beinn Gharbh**.................. bay-n [ben] charv	Rough Hill	
890m 2919ft	**Sgurr Beag**...................... skoor bay-k [beg]	Little Peak	
○ 888m 2913ft	**Sgurr Dhomhnuill** .... skoor don-ool	Donald's Peak...................	889679
○ 887m 2910ft	**Ben Aden** .... ben aa-den	Hill of the Face.................	899986
887m 2910ft	**Stob Coire na Cearc**........ stop cora [korry] na k-yark	Peak of the Hen's Hollow	
○ 885m 2903ft	**Garbh Bheinn**.................. garv vay-n [ven]	Rough Hill	904622
○ 882m 2894ft	**Rois Bheinn** .... rosh vay-n [ven]	Hill of Showers................	756778
○ 882m 2894ft	**Beinn Odhar Bheag**......... bay-n [ben] oh-er bay-k [beg]	Little Dappled Hill	846778
○ 874m 2867ft	**Sgurr na Ba Glaise** .... skoor na baa glasha	Peak of the Grey Cow	771777
873m 2863ft	**An Eag**............................. an ayk	The Notch	
873m 2863ft	**Beinn Odhar Mor** .... bay-n [ben] oh-er more	Big Dappled Hill	
○ 867m 2844ft	**Sgurr na h-Aide** .... skoor na hatch	Peak of the Hat.................	889931
○ 858m 2814ft	**Froach Bheinn** .... frouch vay-n [ven]	Heather Hill......................	986940
855m 2804ft	**Beinn Bhuidhe** .... bay-n voo-ya [ben voo-ee]	Yellow Hill	
○ 853m 2798ft	**Creach Bheinn** .... krech vay-n [ven]	Hill of Spoil......................	871577
852m 2795ft	**Sgurr a'Choire Riabhaich** skoor a chora [korry] ree-vach	Peak of the Speckled Hollow	
○ 849m 2785ft	**Sgurr Ghiubhsachain**....... skoor choov-shach-an	Peak of the Pine Wood	876751
○ 845m 2772ft	**Beinn Resipol** .... bay-n [ben] resh-pol	Homestead Hill	766655
○ 835m 2739ft	**Sgurr Cos na Breachd**...... **Loaigh** skoor kos na bre-cht lou-ch	Peak of the Cave of the..... Speckled Calf	948947
○ 829m 2720ft	**Carn Mor**......................... karn more	Big Hill.............................	903910

Height	Mountain	Translation	Map Ref.
826m 2709ft	**Meall an Tarmachain** ...... me-yal tar-mach-in	Hill of the Ptarmigan	
825m 2706ft	**Beinn Gharbh**................... bay-n [ben] garv	Rough Peak	
817m 2680ft	**Sgurr an Ursainn** .... skoor an oor-san	The Pillar Peak	
815m 2673ft	**Druim a'Chuirn** .... droom [drim] a choorn	Ridge of the Cairn	
○ **814m** 2671ft	**An Stac** .... an stak	The Stack	763794
810m 2657ft	**Beinn an Tuim** .... bay-n [ben] an toom	Hill of Confusion	
○ **796m** 2611ft	**Sgurr nan Utha** .... skoor nan oo-ta	Peak of the Udder.............	885839
790m 2591ft	**Fraoch Bheinn** .... frouch vay-n [ven]	Heather Hill	
787m 2581ft	**Beinn Coire nan Gall** .... bay-n [ben] cora [korry] nan gawl	Hill of the Lowlander's Hollow	
○ **786m** 2579ft	**Carn Nathrach**.................. karn na-trach	Hill of the Serpents...........	887699
○ **783m** 2569ft	**Beinn Mhic Ceididh** .... bay-n [ben] vik kee-ya	Son of Cedidh's Hill..........	829787
○ **775m** 2543ft	**Sgorr Craobh a'Chaorainn** skoor krouv a chou-ran	Peak of the Rowan Tree....	895757
773m 2535ft	**Beinn a'Chaorainn**........... bay-n [ben] a chou-ran	Hill of the Rowan Tree	
770m 2526ft	**Bealach an Sgriodain** ...... b-yal-ach an skree-tan	Pass of the Stony Ravine	
○ **770m** 2526ft	**Druim Tarsuinn**................ droom [drim] tar-sin	Transverse Ridge	875727
○ **765m** 2509ft	**Braigh nan Uamhachan**... bray nan oo-vach-an	Slope of the Caves............	975867
○ **762m** 2499ft	**Beinn na h-Uamha**........... bay-n [ben] na hoo-ava	Hill of the Cave	917664
759m 2489ft	**Meall Mor** .... me-yal more	Big Hill	
755m 2476ft	**Meall nan Creag Leac** ..... me-yal nan kray-k l-ye-cht [le-cht]	Hill of the Rocky Slab	
751m 2463ft	**Diollaid Beag**................... jeel-lat bay-k [beg]	Small Saddle	
750m 2460ft	**Garbh Beinn**..................... garv bay-n [ben]	Rough Hill	
749m 2457ft	**Sgurr an Fhuarain Duibh** . skoor an foor-an doo	Peak of the Black Well	
747m 2450ft	**Sgurr nan Mheirleach**...... skoor nan veerl-yach	Peak of the Thief	

Height	Mountain	Translation
740m 2427ft	**Meall a'Choire Dhuibh** .... me-yal a chora [korry] doo	Hill of the Black Hollow
730m 2394ft	**Sgurr na h-Eanchainne** .... skoor na h-yan-cha-na	Peak of Brains
728m 2388ft	**Sgurr Breac** .... skoor brechk [breck]	Speckled Peak
722m 2368ft	**Meall nan Damh** .... me-yal nan dav	Hill of the Stag
718m 2355ft	**An Stac** .... an stak	The Stack
713m 2339ft	**Sgurr Dhomhuill Mor** .... skoor don-ool more	Big Peak of Donald
710m 2329ft	**Meith Bheinn** .... me vay-n [ven]	Sappy Hill
706m 2316ft	**Sgorr a'Chuir** .... skor a choor	Place of the Snow
701m 2299ft	**Teanga Chorrach** .... t-yen-ga chor-rach	Precipitous Tongue
701m 2299ft	**Sgurr nan Cnamh** .... skoor na krav	Peak of Chew
691m 2266ft	**Na h-Uamhachan** .... na hoo-vach-an	The Caves
687m 2253ft	**Meall a'Chuilinn** .... me-yal a chool-in	Corner Hill
683m 2240ft	**Sron Liath** .... srawn lee-ah	Grey Point
668m 2191ft	**Meall Doire na Matha** ..... me-yal dor-ee [dora] na mah	Hill of the Wife's Thicket
666m 2184ft	**Beinn Gaire** .... bay-n [ben] gare	Laughing Hill
665m 2181ft	**Diollaid Bheag** .... jeel-lak vay-k [beg]	Little Saddle
663m 2175ft	**Aodann Chleireig** .... ou-tan chler-ek	Clergyman's Face
663m 2175ft	**Croit Bheinn** .... krawt vay-n [ven]	Croft Hill
636m 2086ft	**Glas Bheinn** .... glas vay-n [ven]	Green Hill
634m 2079ft	**Meall a'Choire Chruinn** ... me-yal a chora [korry] chroon	Hill of the Rounded Hollow
633m 2076ft	**Glas Charn** .... glas charn	Green Peak
625m 2050ft	**Beinn an t-Snechda** .... bayn an t-rech-ta [ben an sh-nech-ta]	Hill of Snow
612m 2007ft	**Sgurr Mor** .... skoor more	Big Peak

111

41 Ben Nevis
(42 Munros)
(14 Corbetts)

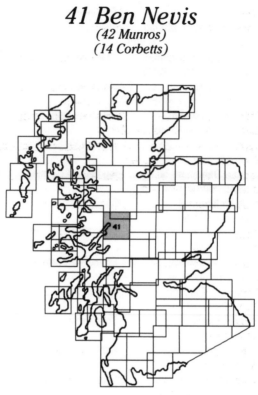

© Crown Copyright

41 BEN NEVIS

Height	Mountain	Translation	Map Ref.
❑ **1344m** 4409ft	**Ben Nevis** ben ne-vis	Venomous Mountain	166713
❑ **1234m** 4048ft	**Aonach Beag** ou-nach bay-k [an-ach beg]	Little Mountain	196715
❑ **1223m** 4012ft	**Carn Mor Dearg** karn more je-rak	Big Red Mountain	177722
❑ **1221m** 4006ft	**Aonach Mor** ou-nach [an-ach] more	Big Mountain	193730
1212m 3975ft	**Carn Dearg** karn jer-ak	Red Hill	
1180m 3870ft	**Carn Dearg Meadhonach** karn jer-ak mee-yon-ach	Middle Red Hill	
❑ **1177m** 3861ft	**Stob Coire Claurigh** stop cora [korry] klaw-ree	Peak of the Brawling Hollow	262739
❑ **1150m** 3773ft	**Bidean nan Bian** beet-yan nan b-yan	Pinnacle of the Mountains (known locally as bid-ee-an)	143542

112

Height	Mountain	Translation	Map Ref.
❑ 1128m 3701ft	**Binnien Mor** .... bin-yan more	Big Peak	212663
1121m 3677ft	**Stob Coire na Ceannain** stop cora [korry] k-yan-an	Peak of the Hollow of the Heads	
❑ 1116m 3661ft	**Stob Coire Easain** .... stop cora [korry] es-an	Peak of the Hollow .... of the Waterfall	308730
❑ 1115m 3658ft	**Stob Coire an Laoigh** .... stop cora [korry] an lou-ch	Peak of the Hollow of the Calf	240725
1115m 3658ft	**Stob Coire nan Lochan** .... stop cora [korry] nan loch-an	Peak of the Hollow of the Little Loch	
❑ 1114m 3655ft	**Aonach Beag**.................... ou-nach bay-k [an-ach beg]	Little Mountain	458742
❑ 1108m 3635ft	**Meall a'Bhuiridh**.............. me-yal a voo-ree	Hill of the Bellowing	251503
1107m 3631ft	**Meall Coire nan Beith** ..... me-yal cora [korry] nan bee	Hill of the Hollow of the Birches	
❑ 1106m 3629ft	**Stob Coire nan Mheadhoin** stop cora [korry] nan vee-yon	Peak of the Middle Hollow	316736
❑ 1100m 3609ft	**Criese** .... kreesh	Greasy Lump	238507
❑ 1100m 3609ft	**Beinn Eibhinn** .... bay-n [ben] ay-vin	Delightful Mountain..........	449733
❑ 1099m 3606ft	**Sgurr a'Mhaim**................. skoor a vaym	Peak of the Rounded Hill ..	165667
❑ 1095m 3592ft	**Sgurr Choinnich Mor** .... skoor chon-yeech more	Big Peak of the Moss........	227714
1070m 3510ft	**Stob Coire Sgreachach**.... stop cora [korry] skree-yach	Peak of the Fearful Hollow	
❑ 1055m 3461ft	**Na Gruagaichean**............. na groo-yach-an	The Maidens.....................	203652
❑ 1052m 3451ft	**Beinn a'Chaorainn**........... bay-n [ben] a chou-ran	Hill of the Rowan Tree......	386851
❑ 1047m 3435ft	**Chno Dearg**...................... ch-naw je-rak	Red Hill.............................	377741
❑ 1032m 3386ft	**Am Bodach** .... am botach	The Old Man.....................	176651
	Beinn a'Bheithir .... bay-n [ben] a vee-hir Highest peak:	Mountain of the Thunderbolt	
❑ 1024m 3360ft	**Sgurr Dearg** .... skoor jer-ak	Red Peak	056558
	Buachaille Etive Mor .... booch-al e-tiv more Highest peak:	Big Herdsman of Etive	
❑ 1022m 3353ft	**Stob Dearg**...................... stop jer-ak	Red Peak	223543

113

Height	Mountain	Translation	Map Ref.
1011m 3316ft	**Stob na Doire**.................. stop na dor-ee [dora]	Peak of the Thicket	
☐ 1008m 3307ft	**Sgurr Eilde Mor** .... skoor eelj more	Big Peak of the Hind........	231658
1007m 3302ft	**Beinn Socach**.................. bay-n [ben] soch-ach	Beak Hill	
☐ 1001m 3284ft	**Sgurr Dhonuill** .... skoor don-ool	Donald's Peak..................	040555
☐ 1001m 3284ft	**Sgor an Iubhair**.............. skoor an yoo-var	Peak of the Yew Tree........	165655
☐ 999m 3277ft	**Stob Ban** .... stop ban	White Peak	148654
☐ 994m 3261ft	**Sgorr na h-Ulaidh**............ skoor na hoo-lay	Peak of the Treasure.........	111518
☐ 987m 3237ft	**Gaor Bheinn or Gulvain** ... gore vay-n [ven]	Dirty Mountain	003876
☐ 982m 3222ft	**An Gearanach** .... an g-yar-an-ach	The Complainer	187670
☐ 981m 3218ft	**Stob Coire a'Chairn** .... stop cora [korry] a charn [kayr-n]	Peak of the Cairn Hollow ..	185661
☐ 977m 3205ft	**Stob Ban** .... stop ban	White Peak	266724
☐ 976m 3202ft	**Stob Coire Sgriodain** .... stop cora [korry] skree-tan	Peak of the Scree Hollow..	356744
	Aonach Eagach .... ou-nach ay-kach [an-ach ee-ah] Highest peak:	Notched Ridge	
☐ 967m 3173ft	**Sgorr nam Fiannaidh**....... skoor nam fee-an-nay	Peak of the Fian Warriors	141583
966m 3169ft	**Sgurr Choinnich Beag**...... skoor chon-yeech bay-k [beg]	Little Peak of the Moss	
965m 3166ft	**Sgurr a'Bhuic**.................. skoor a voo-ik	Peak of the male-goat	
960m 3149ft	**Stob Coire Sgriodain** .... stop cora [korry] skree-tan	Peak of the Scree Hollow	
☐ 959m 3146ft	**Beinn Fhionnlaidh** .... bay-n [ben] fee-on-lay	Finlay's Mountain	095498
	Buachaille Etive Beag ..... booch-al e-tiv bay-k [beg] Highest peak:	Small Herdsman of Etive	
☐ 958ft 3143ft	**Stob Dubh** .... stop doo	Black Peak........................	179535
☐ 955m 3133ft	**Sgor Gaibhre** .... skoor gay-vra	Goat Peak.........................	444674
955m 3133ft	**Stob Coire Broige** .... stop cora [korry] broo-ka	Peak of the Lively Hollow	

Height	Mountain	Translation	Map Ref.
❏ 953m 3127ft	**Meall Dearg**...................... me-yal jer-ak	Red Mountain...................	161584
952m 3123ft	**Beinn Fhada** .... bay-n [ben] fata	Long Hill	
943m 3093ft	**Am Bodach** .... am botach	The Old Man	
❏ 941m 3087ft	**Carn Dearg**...................... karn jer-ak	Red Hill.............................	418661
❏ 940m 3084ft	**Binnein Beag** .... bin-yan bay-k [beg]	Small Peak	222677
940m 3083ft	**Stob Coire Leith**............... stop cora [korry] lay	Peak of the Half Hollow	
❏ 939m 3081ft	**Mullach nam Coirean**...... mool-lach nam kor-an	Summit of the Hollows.....	122662
939m 3081ft	**Stob Coire Altruim**........... stop cora [korry] al-troom	Peak of the Hollow of the Rearing	
❏ 937m 3074ft	**Beinn na Lap** .... bay-n [ben] na laf	Mottled Mountain.............	376696
924m 3031ft	**Stob Coire Raineach**........ stop cora [korry] ran-ach	Peak of the Hollow of the Ferns	
❏ 915m 3002ft	**Beinn Teallach**................ bay-n [ben] t-yeel-lach	Mountain of the Hearth.....	361860
910m 2985ft	**Meall a'Chaorain**............ me-yal a chou-ran	Hill of the Rowan Tree	
○ 907m 2976ft	**Beinn Maol Chaluim**........ bay-n [ben] moul chal-oom	Calum's Bare Mountain	135526
○ 906m 2972ft	**Leum Uilleim**.................... le-oom ool-yam	William's Leap..................	331641
○ 879m 2884ft	**Fraochaidh**....................... frou-chay	Heather Hill.......................	029517
876m 2873ft	**Beinn a'Bhric** .... bay-n [ben] a vrik	Hill of the Trout	
874m 2867ft	**Sron Garbh**...................... srawn garv	Rough Point	
○ 867m 2844ft	**Garbh Bheinn**.................. garv vay-n [ven]	Rough Hill	169601
866m 2841ft	**Meall Garbh**..................... me-yal garv	Rough Hill	
○ 864m 2834ft	**Beinn MhicChasgaig**....... bay-n [ben] vic chas-kay-k	MacCaskaig's Hill	221502
858m 2814ft	**Garbh Beinn**..................... garv bay-n [ben]	Rough Hill	
○ 857m 2811ft	**Beinn a'Chrulaiste**........... bay-n [ben] a chroo-lash-ta	Rocky Hill.........................	246567
○ 857m 2811ft	**Cruach Innse**.................... kroo-ach en-sha	Rocky Peak of the Meadow	280763

Height	Mountain	Translation	Map Ref.
847m 2778ft	**Beinn Maol Chaluim**........ bay-n [ben] moul cha-loom	Calum's Bare Hill	
845m 2772ft	**Aonach Dubh a'Ghlinne**... ou-nach [an-ach] doo a chlena	Black Ridge of the Glen	
840m 2755ft	**Meall a'Bhuirich**............. me-yal a voo-reech	Hill of the Bellowing	
834m 2736ft	**Carn Dearg**...................... karn jer-ak	Red Hill	
817m 2680ft	**Meall a'Mheanbh-Chruidh** me-yal a veen-av chrooy	Hill of the Little Horse Shoe	
815m 2673ft	**Meall Chaorach** .... me-yal chou-rach	Hill of the Sheep	
○ 808m 2650ft	**Sgurr Innse** .... skoor en-sha	Peak of the Meadow.........	290748
○ 796m 2612ft	**Mam na Gualainn** .... mam na gool-an	Round Hill of the Shoulder	115625
○ 796m 2612ft	**Beinn Bhan** .... bay-n [ben] van	White Hill...........................	141857
○ 789m 2588ft	**Glas Bheinn** .... glas vay-n [ven]	Green Hill	259641
○ 774m 2539ft	**Meall a'Phubill**............... me-yal foo-bill	Hill of the Tent...................	029854
○ 772m 2532ft	**Meall Lighiche**................ me-yal lee-yeech	Doctor's Hill	095529
○ 771m 2529ft	**Stob Coire a'Chearcail** .... stop cora [korry] a ch-yar-kal	Peak of the Circular Hollow	017727
764m 2506ft	**Beinn na Callich** .... bay-n [ben] na kal-yeech	Hill of the Old Woman	
749m 2457ft	**Creag Dhubh**.................... kray-k doo	Black Peak	
744m 2440ft	**Stob a'Ghrianain** .... stop a chree-an-an	Hill of the Sunny Spot	
742m 2434ft	**Sgurr na Ciche**................. skoor na keesh-ta	Peak of the Breast	
739m 2424ft	**Stob na Cruaiche** .... stop na kroo-acha	Peak of the Peat Stack	
730m 2395ft	**Sgurr na h-Eanchainne**.... skoor na h-yanch-ayn	Peak of Brains	
729m 2391ft	**Coire an Fhuidhir**............ cora [korry] an foo-yir	Hollow of the Fugitive	
727m 2385ft	**Mullach Coire nan Geur-Oirean** mool-lach cora [korry] nan gear oor-yan	Summit of the Hollow of the Sharp Edge	
722m 2368ft	**Sgurr an Iubhair** .... skoor an yoo-var	Peak of the Yew Tree	

Height	Mountain	Translation
722m 2368ft	**Creaga a'Chaise** .... kray-k a chasha	The Steep Rock
721m 2365ft	**Beinn Chlianaig** .... bay-n [ben] chlee-an-ay-k	Hill of the Meadow
719m 2358ft	**Creag Tharsuinn** .... kray-k tar-sinn	Transverse Hill
718m 2355ft	**Meall Mor** .... me-yal more	Big Hill
711m 2332ft	**Meall an t-Suidhe**............ me-yal an too-ya [soo-ya]	Hill of the Sitting
708m 2322	**Meall Bhalach** .... me-yal va-lach	Hill of the Boy
706m 2316ft	**Stob Mhic Mhartuin**......... stop vic var-toon	Son of Martin's Peak
699m 2293ft	**Meall Cumhann** .... me-yal koo-van	Narrow Hill
698m 2290ft	**Druim Gleann Laoigh** ...... droom [drim] glen lou-ch	Ridge of the Calf Glen
691m 2266ft	**Gearr Aonach**................... g-yar ou-nach [an-ach]	Ridge of the Steep Slope
686m 2250ft	**Meall Onfhaidh**................ me-yal on-fay	Hill of Fury
685m 2247ft	**Leana Mhor** .... lee-ana voar	Big Meadow
679m 2227ft	**Meall an Aodainn** .... me-yal an ou-tan	Hill of the Face
678m 2224ft	**Leana Mhor** .... lee-ana voar	Big Meadow
676m 2217ft	**Meall Mor** .... me-yal more	Big Hill
664m 2178ft	**Beinn na Cloiche** .... bay-n [ben] na kloy-cha	Hill of Stone
663m 2175ft	**Sgorr a'Choise**................. skoor a chosha	Foot-shaped Peak
658m 2158ft	**Creag Dhubh**.................... kray-k doo	Black Peak
654m 2145ft	**Coire Ceirsle**.................... cora [korry] keer-sla	Clew Hollow
639m 2096ft	**Stob Beinn a'Chrulaiste** .. stop bay-n [ben] a chrool-ash-t	Peak of the Rocky Hill
635m 2083ft	**Coille Mhor**...................... kool-a [kolly] voar	Big Woodside
621m 2037ft	**Tom Meadhoin** .... toam [tom] mee-yon	Middle Mound
616m 2020ft	**Beinn na Gucaig** .... bay-n [ben] na goo-kak	Bell-shaped Hill

42 Glen Garry

(19 Munros)
(9 Corbetts)

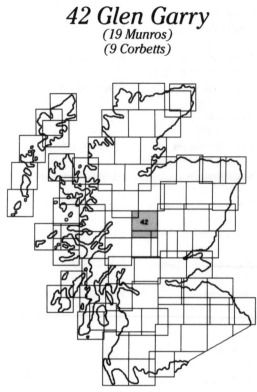

© Crown Copyright

42 GLEN GARRY

	Height	Mountain	Translation	Map Ref.
❑	**1148m** 3766ft	**Ben Alder** ben al-der	Rock Water Mountain	496718
❑	**1132m** 3714ft	**Geal Charn** g-yal charn	White Mountain	470746
❑	**1130m** 3707ft	**Creag Meagaidh** kray-k meg-ay	Bogland Rock	418875
❑	**1114m** 3655ft	**Aonach Beag** ou-nach bay-k [an-ach beg]	Little Mountain	458742
❑	**1100m** 3609ft	**Beinn Eibhinn** bay-n [ben] ay-vin	Delightful Mountain	449733
❑	**1088m** 3569ft	**Beinn a'Chlachair** bay-n [ben] chlach-ar	Stonemason's Mountain	471781
❑	**1049m** 3442ft	**Geal Charn** g-yal charn	White Mountain	504812
❑	**1034m** 3392ft	**Carn Dearg** karn jer-ak	Red Mountain	504764

118

Height	Mountain	Translation	Map Ref.
1027m 3369ft	**Meall Coire Choille-Rais**. me-yal cora [korry] chool-a [kolly] rash	Hill of the Hollow of the Wood	
❑ 1019m 3343ft	**Beinn Bheoil** .... bay-n [ben] vi-al	Mountain of the Mouth.....	517717
❑ 1010m 3314ft	**Beinn Udlamainn**............ bay-n [ben] oot-la-man	Gloomy Mountain............	579740
1004m 3293ft	**Meall a'Bharr**................... me-yal a vaar	Hill of the Summit	
993m 3257ft	**An Cearcallach** .... an k-yar-kal-yach	The Hoop	
❑ 991m 3251ft	**Sgairneach Mhor**............ skar-nach voar	Big Stony Hillside	599732
❑ 975m 3199ft	**A'Mharconaich** .... a var-kon-ach	Place of the Horse	604764
955m 3133ft	**Sron Coire na h-Iolaire**.... srawn cora [korry] na h-yool-ir	Point of the Hollow of the Eagle	
❑ 955m 3133ft	**Stob Gaibhre**.................... stob gay-vra	Goat's Peak	444674
❑ 951m 3120ft	**Meall Chuaich** .... me-yal choo-ach	Hill of the Shallow Bowl....	716879
❑ 941m 3087ft	**Carn na Caim**................... karn na kay-m	Mountain of the Curve......	677822
❑ 941m 3087ft	**Carn Dearg**....................... karn jer-ak	Red Mountain...................	418661
❑ 936m 3071ft	**A'Bhuidheanach Bheag** ... a voo-yan-ach vay-k [beg]	Little Yellow Place	661776
929m 3047ft	**Sgor Choinnich** .... skoor chon-yeech	Peak of the Moss	
928m 3044ft	**Glas Mheall Mor**.............. glas ve-yal more	Big Green Hill	
❑ 924m 3031ft	**Creag Pitridh** .... kray-k peet-ree	Petrie's Rock	488814
922m 3024ft	**Diollaid a' Chairn** .... jeel-at a chayr-n	Saddle of the Cairn	
918m 3011ft	**Mam Ban** .... mam ban	White Hill	
❑ 917m 3008ft	**Geal Charn**....................... g-yal charn	White Mountain................	598783
916m 3004ft	**Meall a'Chaorainn**.......... me-yal a chou-ran	Hill of the Rowan Tree	
○ 911m 2989ft	**The Fara**........................... the fa-ra	Shrouded Hill	598844
911m 2989ft	**Meall Liath** .... me-yal lee-ah	Grey Hill	
901m 2955ft	**Beinn a'Chumhainn**......... bay-n [ben] a choo-van	Narrow Hill	

Height	Mountain	Translation	Map Ref.
901m 2955ft	**Sgor Gaibhre** .... skoor gay-vra	Goat's Peak	
900m 2952ft	**Carn Dearg**..................... karn jer-ak	Red Hill	
900m 2952ft	**Meall Garbh**................... me-yal garv	Rough Hill	
897m 2942ft	**Bogha Cloiche** .... bo-cha kloy-ch	Stone Bow	
897m 2942ft	**Meall Cruaidh**................. me-yal kroo-ay	Hard Hill	
❍ 892m 2926ft	**Beinn a'Chuallaich** .... bay-n [ben] a chool-lach	Hill of the Herding	684618
888m 2913ft	**Carn Dearg**..................... karn jer-ak	Red Hill	
881m 2890ft	**Glas Mheall Beag** .... glas ve-yal bay-k [beg]	Little Green Hill	
879m 2883ft	**A'Bhuidheanach** .... a voo-yan-ach	Yellow Place	
❍ 876m 2874ft	**Craig an Loch** .... kray-k an loch	Hill of the Rock of the....... Loch	735807
874m 2867ft	**Meall na Eun** .... me-yal na ayn	Hill of the Bird	
❍ 868m 2848ft	**Meall na Meoig** .... me-yal na me-ok	Hill of Whey.....................	448642
868m 2848ft	**Mullach Coire nan Dearcag** mool-lach cora [korry] nan jer-kag	Red Summit of the Hollow	
865m 2837ft	**Meall a'Bhealaich** .... me-yal a v-yal-aych	Hill of the Pass	
❍ 855m 2805ft	**Stob an Aonaich Mhoir**.... stop an ou-nach [an-ach] voar	Peak of the Big Ridge	537694
852m 2795ft	**Carn a'Bhealaich**............. karn v-yal-ach	Hill of the Pass	
850m 2788ft	**Meallan Buidhe** .... me-yal-lan boo-ya [boo-ee]	Yellow Hill	
850m 2788ft	**Creag an Loch**................. kray-k an loch	Rock of the Loch	
850m 2788ft	**Garbh Mheall**................... garv ve-yal	Rough Hill	
847m 2779ft	**Sron Bhuirich**................... srawn voo-reech	Point of the Bellowing	
❍ 841m 2759ft	**Beinn Mholaich** .... bay-n [ben] vol-ach	Hairy Hill...........................	587655
838m 2749ft	**Meall na Meoig** .... me-yal na me-ok	Hill of Whey	
834m 2736ft	**Meall Odhar Mor** .... me-yal oh-er more	Big Dappled Hill	

Height	Mountain	Translation	Map Ref.
○ 827m 2713ft	**Am Dun** am doon [dun]	Hill Fort	716802
816m 2676ft	**Sron a'Chleirich** srawn a chler-eech	Point of the Clergyman	
○ 803m 2634ft	**The Sow of Atholl** the sow of a-thol	Boar's Hill	624741
802m 2631ft	**Meall Breac** me-yal brechk [breck]	Speckled Hill	
801m 2628ft	**Meall na Brachdlach** me-yal na brach-t-lach	Hill of Broken Trees	
800m 2625ft	**A'Mharconaich** a var-kon-yach	Place of the Horse	
792m 2598ft	**Geal Charn** g-yal charn	White Hill	
791m 2595ft	**Carn Dearg** karn jer-ak	Red Hill	
789m 2588ft	**Beinn Bhoidheach** bay-n [ben] voy-yach	Beautiful Hill	
785m 2575ft	**Creag Dhubh** kray-k doo	Black Rock	
783m 2568ft	**Meall Odhar Aillig** me-yal oh-er ell-ik	Hill of the Speckled Herb	
○ 775m 2543ft	**Meall na Leitreach** me-yal na lee-treech	Hill of the Slopes	639702
774m 2539ft	**Creagan Mor** kray-kan more	Big Rocks	
750m 2460ft	**Am Meadar** am may-tar	The Milk Pail	
750m 2460ft	**Sron Leachd a'Chaorainn** srawn l-yech-t [le-cht] a chou-ran	Slab Point of the Rowan Tree	
746m 2447ft	**Binnien Shuas** bin-yan soo-as	Upper Peak	
743m 2437ft	**Meall nan Eun** me-yal nan ayn	Hill of the Bird	
739m 2424ft	**An Torc** an toork	The Boar	
732m 2401ft	**Meall Doire** me-yal dor-ee [dora]	Hill of the Thicket	
730m 2394ft	**Meall Odhar** me-yal oh-er	Dappled Hill	
715m 2345ft	**Creag a'Mhaigh** kray-k a vay	Peak of May	
685m 2247ft	**Meall Breac** me-yal brechk [breck]	Speckled Hill	
683m 2240ft	**Coire Odhar Mor** cora [korry] oher more	Big Dappled Hollow	

Height	Mountain	Translation
674m 2211ft	**Beinn Eilde** .... bay-n [ben] eelj	Deer Hill
667m 2188ft	**Binnien Shios** .... bin-yan shees	Downward Peak
664m 2178ft	**Druim nan Sac** .... droom [drim] nan sak	Ridge of the Sack
658m 2159ft	**Creag Ruadh** .... kray-k roo-ah	Red Peak
654m 2145ft	**Creag Chean** .... kray-k ch-yan	Rocky Head
653m 2142ft	**Meall nan Sac** .... me-yal nan sak	Hill of the Sack
643m 2109ft	**Creag a'Chuir** .... kray-k a choor	Snow Rock
625m 2050ft	**Sron a'Chlaonaidh** .... srawn a chlou-nay	The Slanting Point
623m 2043ft	**Na Cnapanan** .... na krap-a-nan	The Lumps
612m 2007ft	**Creag a'Mhadaidh** .... kray-k a va-tay	Rock of the Fox

43 Braemar to Blair Atholl
(36 Munros)
(14 Corbetts)

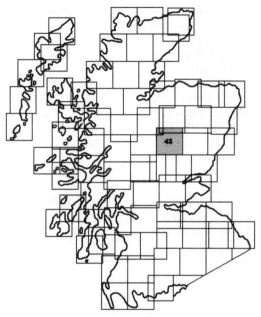

© Crown Copyright

43 BRAEMAR TO BLAIR ATHOLL

	Height	Mountain	Translation	Map Ref.
❑	**1309m** 4295ft	**Ben MacDui** .... ben mak-doo-i	Mountain of the Son of .... Duff	989989
❑	**1296m** 4250ft	**Braeriach** .... bray-reech	Sloping Upper Part...........	953999
❑	**1293m** 4242ft	**Cairn Toul** .... karn [kayr-n] tool	Mountain of the Barn........	963972
	1258m 4126ft	**Sgor an Lochan Uaine** ..... skoor an loch-an oo-ayn	Peak of the Little Green Loch	
❑	**1196m** 3924ft	**Beinn a'Bhuird**................. bay-n [ben] a voort	Mountain of the Table.......	093006
		Ben Avon........................... ben an Highest peak:	River Mountain (Possible translation)	
❑	**1171m** 3842ft	**Leabaidh an Daimh** .... **Bhuidhe** l-ye-pay an dav voo-ya [voo-ee]	Bed of the Yellow Stag	132019

Height	Mountain	Translation	Map Ref.
1157m 3795ft	**Beinn Bhrotain**............... bay-n [ben] vro-tan	Mountain of the Mastiff	954923
1155m 3788ft	**Derry Cairngorm**.............. derry karn gor-om [kayr-n gor-m]	Thicket of the Blue Hill......	017980
	Beinn a'Ghlo .... bay-n ach-lo [ben a-glo] Highest peak:	Mountain of the Mist	
1129m 3704ft	**Carn nan Gobhar**............. karn nan gour	Peak of the Goats	971773
1118m 3668ft	**Sgor Gaoithe**................... skor gou-ee	Peak of the Wind	903989
1113m 3651ft	**Monadh Mor** .... mon-ah more	Big Hill..............................	938942
1110m 3640ft	**Sron Riach** .... srawn ree-ach	Greyish Point	
1089m 3572ft	**Carn Eas**........................... karn es	Waterfall Hill	
1082m 3549ft	**Beinn a'Chaorainn**........... bay-n [ben] a chou-ran	Mountain of the Rowan ....045013 Tree	
1070m 3510ft	**Braigh Coire Chruinn-**...... **Bhalagain** bray cora [korry] chroon vala-kan	Sloping Hollow of the .... Round Lumps	946724
1068m 3503ft	**Glas Maol** .... glas moul	Bare Green Hill	166765
1064m 3491ft	**Cairn of Claise**................. karn [kayr-n] o clay-sh	Hill of the Grassy Hollow ..	185789
1061m 3480ft	**Airgoid Bheinn**................. er-e-kit vay-n [ven]	Silver Hill	
1052m 3451ft	**Carn Ban Mor**................... karn ban more	Large White Hill	
1051m 3448ft	**Glas Tulaichean**............... glas tool-ach-an	Greenish Hillocks	051760
1047m 3434ft	**Carn an t-Sagairt** .... karn an ta-kar-sht [sa-gart]	Big Mountain of the Priest	208843
1045m 3428ft	**Beinn Iutharn Mhor**.......... bay-n [ben] yoo-harn voar	Big Mountain of Hell.........	045792
1037m 3401ft	**Carn a'Mhaim**................... karn a vay-m	Rounded Mountain...........	994952
1029m 3375ft	**Carn an Righ**..................... karn an ree	Mountain of the King........	028773
1019m 3342ft	**Mullach Clach a'Bhlair**.... mool-lach klach av-laar	Summit of the Stony Plain	883927
1019m 3342ft	**Carn an Tuiric** .... karn an toork	Mountain of the Boar........	174804
1008m 3307ft	**Beinn Dearg**..................... bay-n [ben] jer-ak	Red Mountain...................	853778

Height	Mountain	Translation	Map Ref.
❑ 1006m 3300ft	An Sgarsoch..................... an skar-soch	Place of the Sharp Rocks	933836
❑ 1004m 3293ft	The Devil's Point..............	....	976951
❑ 994m 3260ft	Carn Fhidleir.................... karn fee-ler	Fiddler's Mountain...........	905842
988m 3241ft	Mam nan Cairn................ mam nan kayr-n	Mound of the Cairn	
❑ 987m 3237ft	Creag Leacach................ kray-k lech-tach	Slabby Rock	155745
❑ 975m 3198ft	Carn Liath .... karn lee-ah	Grey Mountain..................	936698
❑ 975m 3198ft	Carn a'Gheoidh................ karn a choo-yee	Mountain of the Goose.....	107767
973m 3191ft	Little Glas Maol............... little glas moul	Little Bare Grey Hill	
❑ 963m 3159ft	Carn a Chlamain.............. karn a chla-man	Mountain of the Buzzard...	916758
961m 3152ft	Druim Mor .... droom [drim] more	Big Ridge	
❑ 958m 3143ft	Tolmount .... toal-mun	Valley Hill	210800
❑ 957m 3140ft	Tom Buidhe .... toam boo-ya [tom boo-ee]	Yellow Mound	214788
953m 3126ft	Beinn Iutheran Beag........ bay-n [ben] yoo-har-an bay-k [beg]	Little Hill of Hell	
953m 3126ft	Coire Garbhlach.............. cora [korry] garv-lach	Roughish Hollow	
❑ 946m 3104ft	Carn Bhac .... karn vak [bak]	Peat Banks Mountain........	051832
❑ 944m 3096ft	An Socach....................... an soch-ach	The Beak...........................	080800
942m 3090ft	Carn Cloich Mhuilinn....... karn kloy-ch vool-in	Hill of the Mill Stone	
❑ 933m 3060ft	The Cairnwell .... the kayr-n-well	Hill of the Bags	135773
932m 3057ft	Beinn Gharbh................... bay-n [ben] charv	Rough Hill	
❑ 931m 3054ft	Beinn Bhreac .... bay-n vrechk [ben vreck]	Speckled Mountain...........	058971
930m 3051ft	Glas Choire Bhreac.......... glas cora vrechtk [korry breck]	Little Green Hollow	
922m 3024ft	Meall Odhar..................... me-yal oh-er	Dappled Hill	
920m 3018ft	Cairn Bhac .... kayr-n vach	Peat Banks Cairn	

Height	Mountain	Translation	Map Ref.
918m 3012ft	**Tom Dubh** .... toam [tom] doo	Black Mound	
918m 3012ft	**Druim nam Bo**................. droom [drim] nam bo	Ridge of the Cows	
❑ **917m** 3009ft	**Carn Aosda** .... karn ou-sta	Old Mountain...................	134792
917m 3009ft	**Carn Bhinnein**................. karn vin-yan	Mountain Peak	
○ **912m** 2992ft	**Leathad an Taobhain**....... lay-hat an tou-van	Slope of the Rafters..........	822858
○ **912m** 2992ft	**Beinn Bhreac** .... bay-n vrechk [ben vreck]	Speckled Hill.....................	868821
○ **903m** 2963ft	**Beinn Vuirich** .... bay-n [ben] voor-eech	Hill of the Bellowing	997700
○ **901m** 2956ft	**Beinn Mheadhonach**........ bay-n [ben] vee-yon-ach	Middle Hill	880758
○ **900m** 2953ft	**Culardoch** .... kool-ar-doch	Back High Place...............	193988
899m 2949ft	**Cairn Meall Tionail** .... karn [kayr-n] me-yal tee-on-al	Hill of the Gathering Cairn	
899m 2949ft	**Beinn a'Chait**................... bay-n [ben] a chat	Ruffled Hill	
898m 2946ft	**Meall a'Mhuirich**............. me-yal voor-eech	Hill of the Bellowing	
894m 2932ft	**Carn Creagach**................. karn kray-kach	Rocky Hill	
893m 2929ft	**Cnapan Mor** .... krap-an more	Lumpy Hill	
890m 2919ft	**Carn Crom**........................ karn krom	Crooked Hill	
887m 2909ft	**Braigh nan Creagan Breac** bray nan kray-kan brechk [breck]	Hill of the Speckled Rocks	
887m 2909ft	**Sgor Mor**.......................... skoor more	Big Peak	
885m 2902ft	**Elrig ic an Toisich**............ el-rik an tosh-eech	Macintosh's Deer Trap	
883m 2896ft	**Creagan Lochain** .... kray-kan loch-in	Rock of the Little Loch	
882m 2893ft	**Carn Greanhach**............... karn gran-yach	Hairy Hill	
879m 2883ft	**Braigh Sron Ghorn**........... bray srawn chorn	Point of the Sloping Ember	
878m 2880ft	**Geal Charn**....................... g-yal charn	White Hill	
876m 2873ft	**Carn Mor**.......................... karn more	Big Hill	

Height	Mountain	Translation	Map Ref.
871m 2857ft	**Carn Chlarsaich**............... karn chlar-sach	Harp Hill	
868m 2847ft	**Meall a'Choire Bhuidhe** .. me-yal a cora voo-ya [korry voo-ee]	Hill of the Yellow Hollow	
868m 2847ft	**Carn Dubh**......................... karn doo	Black Hill	
864m 2834ft	**Carn Ait**............................ karn ayt	Joyfull Hill	
○ 862m 2827ft	**Carn Liath** .... karn lee-ah	Grey Hill	165977
859m 2818ft	**Carn an t-Sionnaich**......... karn an te-on-nach [she-on-ach]	Hill of the Fox	
○ 859m 2818ft	**Morrone** .... mor-rone	Big Hill............................	132866
○ 857m 2811ft	**Carn Dearg Mor** .... karn jer-ak more	Big Red Hill	824912
853m 2798ft	**Sron Gharbh**..................... srawn garv	Rough Point	
849m 2785f	**Carn an Fhidhleir Lorgaidh** karn an fee-ler lork-ay	Hill of the Fiddler's Track	
849m 2785ft	**Meall an Uillt Chreagaich** me-yal an oolt chray-kach	Hill of the Rocky Stream	
849m 2785ft	**Meall an t-Slugain**.......... me-yal an t-loo-gan [sloo-gan]	Hill of the Gorge	
○ 841m 2759ft	**Ben Vrackie** .... ben vra-ki	Speckled Hill.....................	951632
841m 2759ft	**Creag Easgaidh** .... kray-k es-kay	Speedy Hill	
○ 834m 2736ft	**Creag nan Gabhar**............ kray-k nan gour	Rock of the Goats.............	154841
822m 2696ft	**Carn Dubh**......................... karn doo	Black Hill	
○ 818m 2683ft	**Carn na Drochaide**........... karn na droch-at	Hill of the Bridge...............	127938
818m 2683ft	**Carn Liath** .... karn lee-ah	Grey Hill	
815m 2673ft	**Meall Ruigh Mor**.............. **Thearlaich** me-yal roo-ya more t-yer-lach	Hill of Charlie's Big Slope	
814m 2670ft	**Sron na Gaoithe**............... srawn na gou-ee	Point of the Wind	
○ 813m 2667ft	**Sgor Mor**.......................... skoor more	Big Rocky Peak	006914
807m 2647ft	**Carn Fiaclach**................... karn fee-a-klach	Toothed Hill	

	Height	Mountain	Translation	Map Ref.
○	807m 2647ft	**Monamenach** mon-a-men-ach	Moorland Hill	176707
○	806m 2644ft	**Ben Gulabin** ben gool-a-bin	Hill of the Curlew	101722
	806m 2644ft	**Carn Torcaidh** karn tork-ay	Hill of the Wild Boars	
	804m 2637ft	**Creag a'Mhadaidh** kray-k a va-tay	Peak of the Fox	
	802m 2631ft	**Creag Bhreac** kray-k vrechk [vreck]	Speckled Hill	
	801m 2628ft	**Ben Earb** ben erp	Hill of the Roe Dee	
	795m 2607ft	**Braigh Coire Caochan na Laogh** bray cora [korry] kou-chan na lou-ch	Sloping Hollow of the Blind Calf	
	794m 2604ft	**Meall Uaine** me-yal oo-ayn	Green Hill	
	789m 2588ft	**Carn Dearg** karn jer-ak	Red Hill	
	788m 2585ft	**Uchd a'Chlarsair** ooch-t a chlar-sar	Minstrel's Point	
	786m 2578ft	**Carn Dearg** karn jer-ak	Red Hill	
	784m 2572ft	**Carn Damhaireach** karn dav-ar-eech	Hill of the Deer Pasture	
	784m 2572ft	**Leachdann Feith Seasgachain** lech-tan fee shes-kach-an	Tomb of the Quiet Cattle	
	784m 2572ft	**Carn Eag Dhubh** karn ayk doo	Hill of the Black Notch	
	782m 2565ft	**Meall Odhar Ailleag** me-yal oh-er al-lay-k	Hill of the Speckled Jewel	
	774m 2539ft	**Creag nan Gobhar** kray-k nan gour	Peak of the Goat	
	774m 2539ft	**Scarsoch Breac** skar-soch brechk [breck]	Little Sharp Rocks	
	771m 2529ft	**Coire na Creige** cora [korry] na kree-ka	Hollow of the Rock	
	770m 2526ft	**Creag na Gaibhre** kray-k na gay-vra	Roughish Rock	
	768m 2519ft	**Carn Aig Mhala** karn ak val-a	Hill of the Near Edge	
	759m 2490ft	**Meall Gorm** me-yal gor-om	Blue Hill	
	759m 2490ft	**Meall Charran** me-yal char-ran	Dwarf Hill	

Hill walking for all ages (G. Cuthbert)

Aonach Mor, Nevis Range – Map 41 (G. Cuthbert)

Glen Nevis – Map 41 (G. Cuthbert)

Hill walking for all ages (G. Cuthbert)

Winter expedition, Ben Lawers – Map 51 (G. Cuthbert)

Winter skills training on Ben Lui – Map 50 (G. Cuthbert)

An Caisteal – Map 50/56 (G. Cuthbert)

Loch Lomond from Ben Vorlich – Map 51/56 (J. Cuthbert)

Caisteal A'Bhail, Isle of Arran – Map 69 (G. Cuthbert)

Goat Fell, Isle of Arran – Map 69 (B. Robertson)

Harry Lawrie Memorial, Ben Ledi – Map 57 (G. Cuthbert)

Height	Mountain	Translation
755m 2476ft	**Carn an Daimh**.................. karn an dav	Hill of the Stag
745m 2443ft	**Buachaille Breige**............ booch-al breeka	Herdsman's Wig
744m 2440ft	**Mount Blair**...................... mun blay-r	Hill of the Field
741m 2430ft	**Sgor Dubh**........................ skoor doo	Black Peak
738m 2421ft	**Craigenloch Hill**.............. kray-kan loch hill	Hill of the Loch of Rocks
737m 2417ft	**Carn na Criche**................ karn na kreech	Hill of the Boundary
737m 2417ft	**Beinn Breac** .... bay-n brechk [ben breck]	Speckled Hill
735m 2411ft	**Sron Saobhaidhe**............ srawn sou-vay	Point of the Fox's Den
733m 2404ft	**Sron na Ban-Righ** .... srawn na ban ree	Point of the Fair King
727m 2385ft	**Sron na Faiceachan**......... srawn na fay-yach-an	Point of the Sharp Eyed
726m 2381ft	**Carn na Craoibhe Seileich** karn na krouv shel-ach	Hill of the Willow Tree
722m 2368ft	**Creagan Garbh**................ kray-kan garv	Rough Rocks
716m 2348ft	**Carn Ban Beag**................ karn ban bay-k [beg]	Small White Hill
712m 2335ft	**Slochd Beag** .... slocht bay-k [beg]	Small Pit
712m 2335ft	**Meall Tionail** .... me-yal tee-on-al	Hill of the Gathering
709m 2326ft	**Meikle Elrick**................... mee-kill el-rik	Big Deer Trap
708m 2323ft	**Creag Phadruig**............... kray-k fa-droog	Patrick's Rock
708m 2323ft	**Meall na h-Eilrig**............. me-yal na h-el-rik	Hill of the Deer Trap
706m 2316ft	**Carn Mor**......................... karn more	Big Hill
694m 2276ft	**Coire Buidhe**................... cora boo-ya [korry boo-ee]	Yellow Hollow
694m 2276ft	**Carn Dearg Beag** .... karn jer-ak bay-k [beg]	Small Red Hill
692m 2269ft	**Dun Mor**.......................... doon [dun] more	Big Fort
691m 2266ft	**Meall Glasail Beag**.......... me-yal glash-al bay-k [beg]	Small Greyish Hill

Height	Mountain	Translation
686m 2250ft	**Meall Odhar**...................... me-yal oh-er	Dappled Hill
676m 2217ft	**Meall Glasil Mor**.............. me-yal glash-al more	Big Greyish Hill
675m 2214ft	**Meall Breac** .... me-yal brechk [breck]	Speckled Hill
674m 2211ft	**Cnapan Garbh**.................. krap-an garv	Rough Lumps
672m 2204ft	**Stac nan Bodach**.............. stak nan botach	Pillar of the Old Man
669m 2194ft	**Sron Chrion a'Bhachin** .... srawn chron a vach-in	Point of the Bank of Danger
667m 2188ft	**Creag a'Chaise** .... kray-k a chash	Steep Rocks
664m 2178ft	**Creag Dhearg**................... kray-k jer-ak	Red Rock
650m 2132ft	**Creag a'Chleirich**............. kray-k a chler-eech	Clergyman's Rock
649m 2129ft	**Creag a'Chait**................... kray-k a chat	Cat's Rock
647m 2122ft	**Meall Reamhar**................ me-yal rav-ar	Fat Hill
638m 2093ft	**Carn Elrig Mor** .... karn el-rik more	Hill of the Big Deer Trap
635m 2083ft	**Creag an t-Sithein** .... kray-k an te-hen [she-hen]	Rock of the Fairy Hill
634m 2080ft	**Carn Mor**.......................... karn more	Big Hill
630m 2066ft	**Carn an Lc'Duibhe**........... karn an doo	The Black Hill
617m 2024ft	**Meall Gorm**...................... me-yal gor-om	Blue Hill
617m 2024ft	**Beinn a'Chruachain**......... bay-n [ben] a chroo-ach-an	Stacky Hill
616m 2020ft	**Aonach Mor** .... ou-nach [an-ach] more	Big Ridge

44 Ballater and Glen Clova
(10 Munros)
(3 Corbetts)

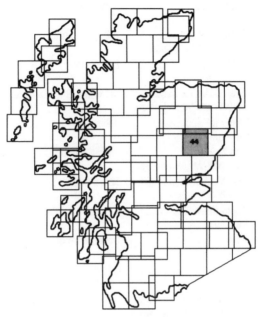

© Crown Copyright

44 BALLATER AND GLEN CLOVA

Height	Mountain	Translation	Map Ref.
❑ 1155m 3789ft	**Lochnagar**...................... loch-na-gar	Little Noisy Loch .... (named after the loch nearby)	244862
	White Mounth .... white munth Highest peak:	The White Mountain	
❑ 1118m 3667ft	**Carn a'Choire Bhoideach** karn a cora [korry] voy-yach	Mountain of the Beautiful . Hollow	226845
1083m 3552ft	**Cuidhe Crom**.................... koo-ya kroam	Crooked Ring of Snow	
1068m 3503ft	**Creag a'Ghlas-uillt**.......... kray-k a chlas oolt	Rock of the Green Stream	
❑ 1047m 3434ft	**Carn an t'Sagairt Mor**...... karn an ta-kar-sht [sa-gart] more	Big Hill of the Priest..........	208843
1044m 3424ft	**Carn an t'Sagairt Beag** .... karn an ta-kar-sht bay-k [sa-gart beg]	Small Hill of the Priest	

Height	Mountain	Translation	Map Ref.
1012m 3320ft	**Cairn Bannoch** .... karn [kayr-n] ban-noch	Mountain of the Cake	223825
1000m 3280ft	**Fafernie** .... fa-fer-nay	Place of the Bog	
998m 3274ft	**Broad Cairn**.....................	Broad Hill	240815
983m 3224ft	**Cairn of Gowal**................. karn [kayr-n] o gowal	Hill of the Fork	
980m 3214ft	**Meikle Pap**....................... me-kil pap	Big Breast	
974m 3194ft	**Meall Coire na Saobhaidhe** me-yal cora [korry] na sou-vay	Hill of the Fox's Den Hollow	
958m 3143ft	**Tolmount** .... toal-mun	Valley Mountain................	210800
957m 3140ft	**Tom Buidhe** .... toam boo-ya [tom boo-ee]	Yellow Mound	214788
947m 3107ft	**Driesh** .... dreesh	Thorn Bush......................	271736
939m 3081ft	**Mount Keen** .... mun keen	Smooth Mountain.............	409869
928m 3045ft	**Mayar**.............................. may-ar	Obscure Mountain............	241738
896m 2940ft	**Ben Tirran**....................... ben teer-ran	Hill of Dry Corn	374746
885m 2902ft	**Meall an Tionail** .... me-yal an tee-on-al	Hill of the Gathering	
876m 2873ft	**Boustie Ley**..................... boo-sti lee	Summer Pastures	
865m 2837ft	**Conachcraig**..................... kon-ach kray-k	Jumbled Rocks................	280865
862m 2827ft	**Caisteal na Callich** .... kash-t-yal na kal-yeech	Castle of the Old Woman	
861m 2824ft	**Creag Liath** .... kray-k lee-ah	Grey Rock	
839m 2572ft	**Cairn Damff** .... karn [kayr-n] dav	Stag Rock	
778m 2552ft	**Mount Battock**.................. mount ba-tock	Small Hill..........................	549845
740m 2427ft	**Badandun**......................... bad-an-doon [dun]	Place of the Fort	
711m 2332ft	**Craig Lair**........................ kray-k lay-r	Mare's Rock	
710m 2329ft	**An t-Sron**......................... an t-rawn [srawn]	The Point	
696m 2283ft	**Monawee** .... mon-a-wee	Yellow Ridge	

47 *Tobermory and North Mull*
(1 Munro)
48 *Iona, Ulva and West Mull*
49 *Oban and East Mull*
(4 Corbetts)

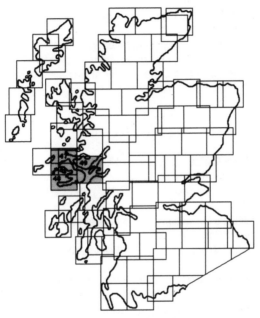

© Crown Copyright

47 NORTH MULL

Height	Mountain	Translation	Map Ref.
❏ **966m** 3168ft	**Ben More** .... ben more	Big Mountain	526331
876m 2844ft	**A'Chioch** .... a chee-och	The Breast	
704m 2309ft	**Cruachan Dearg** .... kroo-ach-an jer-ak	Red Stacks	
702m 2302ft	**Beinn Fhada** .... bay-n [ben] fata	Long Hill	
591m 1938ft	**Beinn Ghraig** .... bay-n [ben] chrayk	Rocky Hill	
572m 1876ft	**Beinn na Gabhar** .... bay-n [ben] na gour	Hill of the Goats	

Height	Mountain	Translation
563m 1846ft	**An Gearna** .... an g-yar-na	The Hare
432m 1417ft	**A'Mhaol Mhor** .... a voul voar	The Big Bare Hill
412m 1351ft	**Beinn Bhuidhe** .... bay-n voo-ya [ben voo-ee]	Yellow Hill
408m 1338ft	**Beinn nan Lus** .... bay-n [ben] nan loos	Hill of the Herbs
376m 1233ft	**Dunan nan Nighean** .... doon-an nan nee-an	The Daughter's Dung-heap
342m 1122ft	**Carn Mor** .... karn more	Big Hill
315m 1033ft	**Beinn nan Clach-Corra** .... bay-n [ben] nan klach cora	Hill of the Stone Hollow

48 WEST MULL

704m 2309ft	**Corra Bheinn** .... cora vay-n [ven]	Hill of the Hollows
618m 2027ft	**Cruach Choireadal** .... kroo-ach cora-dal	Rocky Stacked Hollows
602m 1975ft	**Beinn a'Mheadhon** .... bay-n [ben] a vee-yon	Middle Hill
539m 1768ft	**Sron Dubh** .... srawn doo	Black Point
519m 1702ft	**Beinn na Sreine** .... bay-n [ben] na sreena	Hill of the Bridle
503m 1650ft	**Beinn na Croise** .... bay-n [ben] na krosh	Hill of the Cross
496m 1627ft	**Cruach nan Con** .... kroo-ach nan kon	The Stack of the Dogs
493m 1617ft	**Fionna Mham** .... fee-ona vam	The White Breast
491m 1610ft	**Creach Bheinn** .... krech vay-n [ven]	Hill of Spoil
466m 1528ft	**Beinn nan Feannag** .... bay-n [ben] nan f-yan-nak	Hill of the Hooded Crow
449m 1473ft	**Beinn Charsaig** .... bay-n [ben] char-say-k	Hill of the Plain
435m 1427ft	**Beinn nan Gobhar** .... bay-n [ben] nan gour	Hill of the Goats
432m 1417ft	**Bearraich** .... b-yar-ach	Brow of the Hill
376m 1233ft	**Beinn Chreagach** .... bay-n [ben] chray-kach	Rocky Hill

Height	Mountain	Translation	Map Ref.
376m 1233ft	**Cruach Min** .... kroo-ach meen	Smooth Stack	
375m 1230ft	**Am Binnein** .... am bin-yan	The Peak	
341m 1118ft	**Beinn Chreachan** .... bay-n [ben] chray-chan	Hill of Spoils	
330m 1082ft	**Creachan Mor** .... krech-an more	Big Spoils	

49 OBAN and EAST MULL

OBAN (MAINLAND)

	Height	Mountain	Translation	Map Ref.
○	**853m** 2798ft	**Creach Bheinn** .... krech vay-n [ven]	Hill of Spoil.......................	871577
○	**765m** 2510ft	**Fuar Bheinn** .... foor vay-n [ven]	Cold Hill............................	853564
	739m 2424ft	**Beinn Mheadhoin** .... bay-n [ben] vee-yon	Middle Hill	
	708m 2322ft	**Beinn Breac** .... bay-n brechk [ben breck]	Speckled Hill	
	655m 2148ft	**Meall Ban** .... me-yal ban	White Hill	
	651m 2135ft	**Beinn Na Cille** .... bay-n [ben] na keely	Hill of the Church	
	623m 2043ft	**Glas Bheinn** .... glas vay-n [ven]	Green Hill	

EAST MULL

	Height	Mountain	Translation	Map Ref.
○	**766m** 2512ft	**Dun Da Ghaoithe** .... doon da chou-ee [dun da goo-ee]	Two Winds Fort................	672362
○	**761m** 2496ft	**Beinn Talaidh** .... bay-n [ben] tal-la	Hill of the Good Pasture ...	625347
	754m 2473ft	**Mainnir nan Fiadh** .... man-yir na fee-ay	Pen of the Deer	
	741m 2430ft	**Sgurr Dearg** .... skoor jer-ak	Red Peak	
	714m 2342ft	**Ben Buie** .... ben boo-ee	Yellow Hill	
	698m 2289ft	**Creach Beinn** .... krech bay-n [ben]	Hill of Spoil	
	637m 2089ft	**Beinn Mheadhoin** .... bay-n [ben] vee-yon	Middle Hill	
	633m 2076ft	**Beinn Bhearnach** .... bay-n [ben] veer-nach	Hill of the Gaps	

Height	Mountain	Translation
579m 1899ft	**Beinn Chragach Mhor**...... bay-n [ben] chray-kach voar	Big Rocky Hill
544m 1784ft	**Sgulan Mor**...................... skoolan more	Big Basket
522m 1712ft	**Maol a'Ghearraida**.......... moul ach-yar-da	Bare Pasture
504m 1653ft	**Beinn Chaisgidle**............ bay-n [ben] chash-ki-dil	Easter Hill
501m 1643ft	**Beinn Fhada**................... bay-n [ben] fata	Long Hill
491m 1610ft	**Glas Bheinn**..................... glas vay-n [ven]	Green Hill
429m 1407ft	**Maol nan Uan**................. moul nan oo-an	The Bare Hill of the Lambs
405m 1328ft	**Druim Fata**...................... droom [drim] fata	Long Ridge
377m 1237ft	**Beinn a'Bhainne**............. bay-n [ben] a van-ya	Milk Hill
366m 1200ft	**Maol Buidhe**................... moul boo-ya [boo-ee]	Bare Yellow Hill

50 Glen Orchy
(30 Munros)
(15 Corbetts)

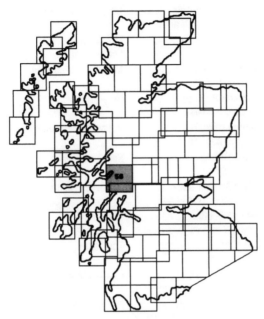

© Crown Copyright

50 GLEN ORCHY

	Height	Mountain	Translation	Map Ref.
❏	**1130m** 3707ft	**Ben Lui** ben loo-i	Mountain of the Calf	266263
❏	**1126m** 3694ft	**Ben Cruachan** ben kroo-ach-an	Stacky Mountain	069304
	1098m 3601ft	**Clach Leathad** klach lay-hat	Stone of the Broad Slope	
❏	**1087m** 3566ft	**Stob Gabhar** stop gour	Goat Peak	230455
❏	**1081m** 3547ft	**Beinn a'Chreachain** bay-n [ben] a chree-ach-an	Mountain of the Rocks	373441
❏	**1078m** 3537ft	**Ben Starav** ben star-av	Stout Mountain	126427
❏	**1076m** 3530ft	**Beinn Dorain** bay-n [ben] dor-an	Mountain of the Streamlet	326378
❏	**1048m** 3438ft	**Creag Mhor** kray-k voar	Big Rock	390361

Height	Mountain	Translation	Map Ref.
1046m 3431ft	**Cruach Ardrain**................ kroo-ach ar-dran	Stack of the High Peak	409211
1044m 3425ft	**Stob Coir'an Albannaich** stop cor-an al-pan-ach	Peak of the Hollow .... of the Scot	169433
1039m 3409ft	**Beinn Achaladair**............ bay-n [ben] ach-al-atir	Mountain of Hard Water ...	346434
1029m 3376ft	**Ben Oss**........................ ben awss	Mountain of the .... Loch-outlet	288253
1025m 3363ft	**Ben Challum**.................. ben chal-loom	Malcolm's Mountain........	387322
1009m 3310ft	**Drochaid Ghlas**............. droch-at chlas	Grey Bridge	
1002m 3287ft	**Beinn Dothaidh**............. bay-n [ben] do-hay	Hill of the Scorching........	332408
998m 3274ft	**Stob Diamh**.................... stop dav	Peak of the Stag	095308
997m 3271ft	**Glas Bheinn Mhor**.......... glas vay-n [ven] voar	Big Green Mountain..........	153429
997m 3271ft	**Meall Buidhe**.................. me-yal boo-ya [boo-ee]	Yellow Hill	
995m 3264ft	**An Caisteal** .... an kash-t-yal	The Castle......................	379193
989m 3245ft	**Beinn Eunaich**.................. bay-n [ben] ayn-yach	Fowling Mountain..............	136328
980m 3215ft	**Beinn a'Chochuill** .... bay-n [ben] a choch-ool	Mountain of the Shell	110328
978m 3208ft	**Beinn Dubhcraig**............... bay-n [ben] doo-kray-k	Mountain of the Black....... Rock	308255
974m 3194ft	**Sron na Giubhas**............... srawn na goo-vash	Point of the Pine Trees	
960m 3150ft	**Beinn nan Aighean** .... bay-n [ben] nan ay-yan	Mountain of the Hinds......	149405
959m 3146ft	**Beinn Fhionnlaidh** .... bay-n [ben] fee-on-lay	Finlay's Mountain	095498
954m 3130ft	**Beinn Mhanach**.................. bay-n [ben] van-ach	Monk's Mountain	373412
948m 3110ft	**Beinn Bhuidhe** .... bay-n voo-ya [ben voo-ee]	Yellow Mountain................	204187
943m 3094ft	**Stob a'Choire Odhair** .... stop a chora [korry] oh-er	Peak of the Dappled .... Hollow	258461
943m 3094ft	**Ben Vorlich** .... ben vor-leech	Mountain of the Bay	295123
941m 3086ft	**Stob a'Bhruaich Leith**...... stop a vroo-ach lay	Peak of the Half Bank	
940m 3084ft	**Beinn a'Chroin**................. bay-n [ben] a chroy-n	Mountain of Danger..........	394186

Height	Mountain	Translation	Map Ref.
939m 3079ft	**Stob a' Bhruaich Leith**..... stop a vroo-ach lay	Peak of the Half Bank	
❏ **937m** 3074ft	**Beinn Sgulaird**................. bay-n [ben] skool-art	Mountain of Shelter..........	053461
❏ **933m** 3061ft	**Beinn Chabhair**................ bay-n [ben] cha-var	Hawk Mountain	367180
❏ **928m** 3045ft	**Meall nan Eun** .... me-yal nan ayn	Mountain of the Bird........	192449
923m 3027ft	**Beinn a'Chuirn**................. bay-n [ben] a choorn	Hill of the Cairn	
❏ **916m** 3005ft	**Beinn a'Chleibh**............. bay-n [ben] a chleev	Mountain of the Chest......	251256
916m 3005ft	**Meall Cuanail** .... me-yal koo-an-al	Hill of the Choir	
○ **907m** 2976ft	**Beinn Maol Chaluim**........ bay-n [ben] moul chal-oom	Calum's Bare Hill..............	135526
906m 2972ft	**Meall nan Each**................ me-yal nan yach	Hill of the Horses	
○ **901m** 2956ft	**Beinn Odhar**...................... bay-n [ben] oh-er	Dappled Hill......................	338339
○ **897m** 2943ft	**Beinn a'Bhuiridh**.............. bay-n [ben] a voo-ree	Hill of the Bellowing	094283
895m 2936ft	**Meall Tionail** .... me-yal tee-on-al	Gathering Hill	
○ **886m** 2907ft	**Beinn a'Chaistel**.............. bay-n [ben] a chash-tyal	Hill of the Castle	348364
○ **885m** 2904ft	**Cam Chreag**..................... kam chray-k	Crooked Rock...................	375346
○ **883m** 2897ft	**Stob Dubh** .... stop doo	Black Peak........................	166488
○ **880m** 2887ft	**Beinn Chuirn**.................... bay-n [ben] choorn	Hill of the Cairn................	281292
876m 2873ft	**Meall Odhar**..................... me-yal oh-er	Dappled Hill	
875m 2870ft	**Meall Tarsuinn** .... me-yal tar-sinn	Transverse Hill	
867m 2844ft	**Aonach Mor** .... ou-nach [an-ach] more	Big Ridge	
○ **864m** 2835ft	**Beinn Mhic Chasgaig** ...... bay-n [ben] vik chas-kay-k	MacChaskaig's Hill	221502
863m 2831ft	**Meall Garbh**..................... me-yal garv	Rough hill	
○ **840m** 2755ft	**Beinn Udlaidh**................. bay-n [ben] oot-lay	Gloomy Hill.......................	280333
○ **839m** 2752ft	**Beinn Trilleachan** .... bay-n [ben] tril-yach-an	Sandpiper Hill...................	086439

Height	Mountain	Translation	Map Ref.
834m 2736ft	**Beinn Taoig** .... bay-n [ben] tou-ik	Passion Hill	
822m 2696ft	**Stob an Duine Ruaidh** ..... stop an don-ya roo-ah	Peak of the Red Man	
○ **818m** 2684ft	**Beinn Chaorach** .... bay-n [ben] chou-rach	Hill of the Sheep	359328
817m 2680ft	**Binnein an Fhidhleir** .... bin-yan an fee-ler	Peak of the Fiddler	
814m 2670ft	**Meall Dhamh** .... me-yal dav	Stag Hill	
○ **810m** 2657ft	**Creach Bheinn** .... krech vay-n [ven]	Hill of Plunder	024422
810m 2657ft	**Meall Copagach** .... me-yal kopa-kach	Hill of the Plants	
○ **806m** 2644ft	**Beinn nan Fuaran** .... bay-n [ben] nan foor-an	Hill of the Wells	361381
803m 2634ft	**Ceann Garbh** .... k-yann garv	Rough Head	
803m 2634ft	**Meall Garbh** .... me-yal garv	Rough Hill	
○ **802m** 2631ft	**Beinn Bhreac Liath** .... bay-n vrechk [ben vreck] lee-ah	Speckled Grey Hill	303339
○ **793m** 2601ft	**Beinn Mhic-Mhonaidh** ..... bay-n [ben] vic vonay	Hill of the Son of the Moor	208349
773m 2535ft	**Beinn Dubh** .... bay-n [ben] doo	Black Hill	
764m 2506ft	**Meall an Fhudair** .... me-yal an foo-tar	Gunpowder Hill	
747m 2450ft	**Meall Mor** .... me-yal more	Big Hill	
739m 2424ft	**Meall nan Tighearn** .... me-yal na ti-yarn	Hill of the Lairds	
734m 2408ft	**Troisgeach** .... troy-skach	Hill of Hunger	
727m 2385ft	**Stob an Duibhe** .... stop an doo	The Black Peak	
722m 2696ft	**Meall nan Caora** .... me-yal nan kou-ra	Hill of the Sheep	
715m 2345ft	**Beinn Lurachan** .... bay-n [ben] loor-ach-an	Pretty Hill	
714m 2342ft	**Beinn Mheadhonach** .... bay-n [ben] vee-yon-ach	Middle Hill	
709m 2325ft	**Beinn nan Lus** .... bay-n [ben] nan loos [luss]	Hill of the Herbs	
708m 2322ft	**Stob Glas** .... stop glas	Green Peak	

Height	Mountain	Translation
708m 2322ft	**Sron Garbh**.............. srawn garv	Rough Point
701m 2299ft	**Meall Garbh**.................. me-yal garv	Rough Hill
697m 2286ft	**Meall an Araich** .... me-yal an ar-eech	Rear Hill
696m 2283ft	**Meall Garbh**.................. me-yal garv	Rough Hill
694m 2276ft	**Beinn an t-Sidhein**........... bay-n an te-yen [ben an she-hen]	Hill of the Fairies
686m 2250ft	**Maol Mor** .... moul more	Bare Hill
684m 2244ft	**Stob Gaibhre**.................... stop gay-vra	Roughish Peak
683m 2241ft	**Beinn Damhain**............... bay-n [ben] dav-an	Stag's Hill
682m 2237ft	**Meall Dubh** .... me-yal doo	Black Hill
676m 2217ft	**Beinn Chas** .... bay-n [ben] chas	Steep Hill
675m 2214ft	**Beinn Suidhe** .... bay-n [ben] soo-ya	Sitting Hill
664m 2178ft	**Meall Tairbh** .... me-yal tay-rv	Advantage Hill
658m 2159ft	**Clachan Hill** .... klach-an hill	Stony Hill
655m 2148ft	**Beinn Bheag** .... bay-n vay-k [ben beg]	Little Hill
653m 2142ft	**Stob an Fhainne** .... stop an fan-nay	Peak of the Rings
651m 2136ft	**Meall Buidher**.................. me-yal boo-yer	Auburn Hill
648m 2125ft	**Beinn Donachain** .... bay-n [ben] don-ach-an	Hill of Badness
645m 2116ft	**Maol Breac** .... moul brechk [breck]	Bare Speckled Hill
641m 2102ft	**Monadh Driseig** .... mon-ah dreesh-k	Thorn Bush Hill
636m 2086ft	**Beinn na Sroine** .... bay-n [ben] na sroy-na	Offended Hill
623m 2043ft	**Meall Buidhe** .... me-yal boo-ya [boo-ee]	Yellow Hill
623m 2043ft	**Meall Riaghain**................. me-yal reech-an	Water Course Hill
621m 2037ft	**Ben Glas** .... ben glas	Green Hill

141

51 Loch Tay
(25 Munros)
(13 Corbetts)

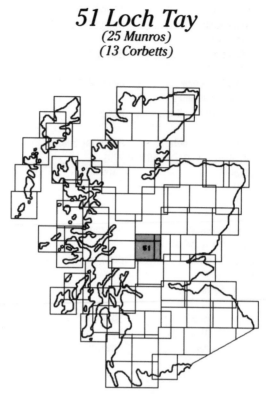

© Crown Copyright

51 LOCH TAY

Height	Mountain	Translation	Map Ref.
❑ **1214m** 3983ft	**Ben Lawers** ben law-ers	Loud Mountain	636414
❑ **1174m** 3852ft	**Ben More** ben more	Big Mountain	432244
❑ **1165m** 3822ft	**Stob Binnein** stop bin-yan	Pinnacle Peak	435227
❑ **1118m** 3668ft	**Meall Garbh** me-yal garv	Rough Mountain	644437
❑ **1103m** 3619ft	**Beinn Ghlas** bay-n [ben] chlas	Green Mountain	626404
❑ **1083m** 3553ft	**Schiehallion** shee-hal-yan	Fairy Hill of the Scots	714548
❑ **1076m** 3530ft	**Ben Heasgarnich** ben hes-kar-neech	Peaceful Mountain	413383
❑ **1069m** 3507ft	**Meall Corranaich** me-yal kor-ra-nach	Mountain of Lament	616410

Height	Mountain	Translation	Map Ref.
1066m 3575ft	**Stob Coire an Lochan** ...... stop cora [korry] an loch-an	Peak of the Hollow of the Loch	
❑ **1048m** 3438ft	**Creag Mhor** .... kray-k voar	Big Rock	390361
❑ **1046m** 3431ft	**Cruach Ardrain** .... kroo-ach ar-dran	Stack of the High Peak	409211
❑ **1043m** 3422ft	**Meall nan Tarmachan** ..... me-yal nan tar-mach-an	Mountain of the Ptarmigan	585390
❑ **1041m** 3415ft	**Carn Mairg** .... karn mayr-k	Mountain of Sorrow	684513
❑ **1039m** 3409ft	**Meall Ghaordaidh** .... me-yal chour-day [gor-day]	Mountain of the Shoulder.	514397
❑ **1028m** 3373ft	**Carn Gorm** .... karn gor-om	Blue Mountain	635501
1004m 3293ft	**Meall a'Bharr** .... me-yal a vaar	Hill of the Top	
❑ **1001m** 3284ft	**Meall Greigh** .... me-yal grey	Mountain of the Horse ...... Studs	674437
❑ **985m** 3232ft	**Ben Vorlich** .... ben vor-leech	Mountain of the Bay	629189
❑ **981m** 3218ft	**Creag Mhor** .... kray-k voar	Big Rock	695496
❑ **975m** 3232ft	**Stuc a'Chroin** .... stook a chroy-n	Peak of Danger	617175
❑ **968m** 3176ft	**Meall Garbh** .... me-yal garv	Rough Mountain	646517
966m 3168ft	**Meall na Dige** .... me-yal na jee-ka	Hill of the Moat	
960m 3150ft	**Stob Garbh** .... stop garv	Rough Peak	
❑ **960m** 3150ft	**Stuchd an Lochain** .... stooch-t an loch-in	Peak of the Little Loch	483448
❑ **960m** 3150ft	**Meall Glas** .... me-yal glas	Green Mountain	431322
937m 3073ft	**Beinn Cheatnaich** .... bay-n [ben] cheen-yach	Misty Hill	
❑ **935m** 3067ft	**Sgiath Chuil** .... skee-ah chool	Back Wing	463318
❑ **932m** 3058ft	**Meall Buidhe** .... me-yal boo-ya [boo-ee]	Yellow Mountain	498499
❑ **931m** 3054ft	**Ben Chonzie** .... ben hon-zay (known locally as Ben-y-Hone)	Mossy Mountain	774309
❑ **926m** 3038ft	**Meall a Choire Leith** .... me-yal a chora [korry] lay	Mountain of the Half .... Hollow	612439
917m 3008ft	**Meall a'Churain** .... me-yal a choo-ran	Hill of the Coarse Cloth	

Height	Mountain	Translation	Map Ref.
912m 2991ft	**Garbh Mheall** garv ve-yal	Rough Hill	
911m 2988ft	**Creag na Caillich** kray-k na kal-yeech	Rock of the Old Woman	
○ 909m 2982ft	**Beinn Oighreag** bay-n [ben] oy-rak	Hill of the Cloud Berries....	543412
○ 907m 2976ft	**Meall Buidhe** me-yal boo-ya [boo-ee]	Yellow Hill	427450
904m 2965ft	**Stob Creagach** stop kray-kach	Rocky Peak	
○ 888m 2913ft	**Creagan na Beinne** kray-kan na bay-na	Hill of the Rocks	744369
887m 2909ft	**Creag an Fheadain** kray-k an fee-tan	Rock of the Stream	
○ 879m 2883ft	**Creag Uchdag** kray-k ooch-tak	Rocky Point	708323
878m 2880ft	**Meall a'Phuill** me-yal a foo-ill	Hill of the Tent	
874m 2867ft	**Meall nan Eun** me-yal nan ayn	Hill of the Birds	
871m 2857ft	**Meall Daill** me-yal dawl	Hidden Hill	
870m 2854ft	**Sron a'Chaoineidh** srawn a chou-nay	Point of the Weeping	
866m 2840ft	**Coire Lobhaibh** cora [korry] lov-ay	Decaying Hollow	
864m 2834ft	**Meall na Samhna** me-yal na sav-na	Hill of the Bonfire	
862m 2829ft	**Beinn a'Bhuic** bay-n [ben] a voo-ik	Hill of the Roe Deer	
○ 862m 2829ft	**Cam Chreag** kam chray-k	Crooked Rock	536491
858m 2814ft	**Meall nan Eanchainn** me-yal nan ayn-chan	Hill of the Cunning	
855m 2804ft	**Stob Cire Bhuidhe** stop keer voo-ya [boo-ee]	Yellow Crested Peak	
○ 852m 2795ft	**Meall an t-Seallaidh** me-yal an t-yal-ay[sh-yal-lay]	Hill of the Viewpoint	542234
851m 2992ft	**Sgiath Chrom** skee-ah chrom	Crooked Wing	
850m 2988ft	**Creag nan Eun** kray-k nan ayn	Rock of the Bird	
○ 849m 2785ft	**Beinn nam Imirean** bay-n [ben] eem-ran	Hill of the Ridge	419309
845m 2772ft	**Meall Cnap-Larnaich** me-yal krap larn-ach	Hill of the Lumpy Ruin	

Height	Mountain	Translation	Map Ref.
842m 2762ft	**Creag nan Lochain** .... kray-k nan loch-in	Rock of the Little Loch	
○ 837m 2746ft	**Sron a'Choire** .... **Chnapanaich** srawn a chora [korry] cha-fa-nich	Point of the Lumpy .... Hollow	456453
837m 2746ft	**Sron nan Eun** .... srawn nan ayn	Point of the Bird	
833m 2732ft	**Stob Glas** .... stop glas	Green Peak	
833m 2732ft	**Meall na Oighreag** .... me-yal na oy-rak	Hill of the Cloud Berries	
○ 830m 2723ft	**Beinn Dearg** .... bay-n [ben] jer-ak	Red Hill	609497
828m 2716ft	**Meall Cruinn** .... me-yal kroon	Round Hill	
813m 2667ft	**Meall Eich** .... me-yal ech	Horse's Hill	
813m 2667ft	**Meall an Odhar** .... me-yal an oh-er	Dappled Hill	
○ 809m 2654ft	**Creag MacRanaich** .... kray-k mak ran-ach	Son of Rannich's Rock	546256
○ 809m 2654ft	**Meall na Fearna** .... me-yal na feer-na	Hill of the Alder Trees	651186
○ 806m 2644ft	**Meall nan Subh** .... me-yal na soov	Hill of the Raspberry	461397
802m 2631ft	**Meall Breac** .... me-yal brechk [breck]	Speckled Hill	
795m 2608ft	**Beinn Bhreac** .... bayn vrechk [ben vreck]	Speckled Hill	
791m 2595ft	**Meall an Fhiodhain** .... me-yal an fee-yan	Hill of the Forest	
790m 2591ft	**Geal Charn** .... g-yal charn	White Cairn	
788m 2585ft	**Meall na Aighean** .... me-yal na ay-yan	Hill of the Deer	
788m 2585ft	**Carn Chois** .... karn chosh	Foot Hill	
○ 779m 2556ft	**Meall nam Maigheach** .... me-yal nam my-ach	Hill of the Hare	586436
779m 2556ft	**Creag Riabhach** .... kray-k ree-vach	Grizzled Rock	
752m 2467ft	**The Stob** .... the stop	The Peak	
745m 2444ft	**Meall a'Mhuic** .... me-yal a vook	Hill of the Pig	

Height	Mountain	Translation
745m 2444ft	**Meall Dhuinn Croisg**........ me-yal doo-in krosh-k	Hill of the Black Cross
734m 2404ft	**Stob Caol** .... stop koul	Narrow Peak
719m 2358ft	**Creag Mhor**..................... kray-k voar	Big Rock
716m 2348ft	**Beinn Bhreac** .... bayn vrechk [ben vrevk]	Speckled Hill
705m 2312ft	**Beinn Leabhain** .... bay-n [ben] l-ye-van	Hill of the Bed
699m 2293ft	**Meall Phubuill** .... me-yal foo-bill	Hill of the Tent
697m 2286ft	**Creag an Sgliata**............. kray-k an sklee-ata	Hill of Slate
682m 2237ft	**Tullich Hill** .... tool-leech hill	Hillock Hill
682m 2237ft	**Ruadh Mheall** .... roo-ah ve-yal	Red Hill
678m 2224ft	**Meall Reamhar**................ me-yal rav-ar	Fat Hill
676m 2217ft	**Meall Gruamach**............. me-yal groo-a-mach	Gloomy Hill
671m 2201ft	**Sron Mhor**........................ srawn voar	Big Point
665m 2181ft	**Meall a'Choire Creagaich** me-yal a chora [korry] kray-kach	Hill of the Rocky Hollow
663m 2175ft	**Meall na Cloiche** .... me-yal na kloy-ch	Hill of the Stone
655m 2148ft	**Meall a'Bhobhuir**............. me-yal a vo-voor	Stranger's Hill
654m 2145ft	**Craig Chean** .... kray-k ch-yan	Rocky Head
653m 2142f	**Meall nan Sac**.................. me-yal nan sak	Hill of the Sack
642m 2106ft	**Creag nan Eideag** .... kray-k nan ee-jay-k	Rock of Armour
640m 2099ft	**Mor Bheinn** .... more vay-n [ven]	Big Hill
640m 2099ft	**Eildeach**........................... eel-yach	Abounding with Deer
637m 2089ft	**Creag Ghrabh**.................. kray-k garv	Rough Rock
628m 2060ft	**Creagan na Gobhar**.......... kray-kan na gour	Little Goat Rock
626m 2053ft	**Creag nan Speireag**......... kray-k nan speer-ay-k	Rock of the Sparrow Hawks

52 Pitlochry to Crieff
(1 Munro)
(5 Corbetts)

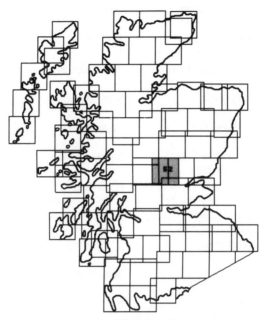

© Crown Copyright

52 PITLOCHRY TO CRIEFF

Height	Mountain	Translation	Map Ref.
❑ **931m** 3054ft	**Ben Chonzie**...................... ben hon-zay (known locally as Ben-y-Hone)	Mossy Mountain...............	773309
○ **888m** 2913ft	**Creagan na Beinne**.......... kray-kan na bay-na	Hill of the Rocks...............	744369
874m 2867ft	**Meall na Eun** .... me-yal ayn	Hill of the Bird	
870m 2854ft	**Sron a'Chaoineidh**........... srawn a choun-ay	Point of the Weeping	
858m 2814ft	**Meall nan Eanachan**........ me-yal nan ayn-ach-an	Hill of the Cunning	
852m 2785ft	**Creag nan Eun** .... kray-k nan ayn	Rock of the Bird	
○ **841m** 2759ft	**Ben Vrackie** .... ben vra-ki	Speckled Hill......................	951632
833m 2732ft	**Meall nan Oighreag**......... me-yal nan oy-rak	Hill of the Cloud Berries	

Height	Mountain	Translation	Map Ref.
819m 2686ft	**Creag Gharbh**.................. kray-k garv	Rough Hill	
805m 2640ft	**Meall nan Fuaran** .... me-yal nan foor-an	Hill of the Well	
○ **789m** 2588ft	**Auchnafree Hill**............... awch-na-free hill	Deer Forest Hill.................	808308
787m 2582ft	**Choinneachain Hill**.......... chon-yach-an hill	Mossy Hill	
○ **787m** 2582ft	**Meall Tairneachan** .... me-yal tayr-nach-an	Hill of Thunder..................	807544
786m 2578ft	**Carn Chois** .... karn chosh	Foot Hill	
○ **783m** 2568ft	**Farragon Hill** .... far-a-gon hill	Feargain's Hill...................	840553
774m 2539ft	**Auchnafree Craig**............ auch-na-free kray-k	Deer Forest Rock	
730m 2394ft	**Beinn na Gainimh**........... bay-n [ben] na gan-iv	Hill of Sand	
725m 2378ft	**Sron Bealaidh**.................. srawn b-yal-ay	Point of the Broom	
716m 2348ft	**Beinn Bhreac** .... bay-n vrechk [ben vreck]	Speckled Hill	
697m 2286ft	**Creag an Sgliata**.............. kray-k an sklee-ata	Rock of Slate	
690m 2263ft	**Meall Dearg**...................... me-yal jer-ak	Red Hill	
689m 2260ft	**Beinn Eargach** .... bay-n [ben] ayr-kach	Angry Hill	
682m 2237ft	**Tullich Hill**....................... tool-leech hill	Little Hill	
667m 2188ft	**Meall Reamhar**................ me-yal ra-var	Lumpy Hill	
665m 2181ft	**Meall a'Choire Chreagaich** me-yal a chora [korry] chray-kach	Hill of the Rocky Hollow	
665m 2181ft	**Geal Charn**....................... g-yal charn	White Hill	
663m 2175ft	**Creag an Lochan**............. kray-k an loch-an	Rock of the Little Loch	
654m 2145ft	**Creag Chean** .... kray-k ch-yan	Rocky Head	
648m 2125ft	**Meall Tarsuinn** .... me-yal tar-sinn	Transverse Hill	
640m 2099ft	**Mor Bheinn** .... more vay-n [ven]	Big Hill	
631m 2070ft	**Meall Dun Dhomhuill** ...... me-yal doon [dun] don-ool	Donald's Fort Hill	

Height	Mountain	Translation
623m 2043ft	**Meall na Caorach** .... me-yal na kou-rach	Hill of the Sheep
617m 2024ft	**Meall a'Charra** .... me-yal a char-ra	Monument Hill
617m 2024ft	**Meall Reamhar** .... me-yal ra-var	Fat Hill
616m 2021tf	**Creag Choille** .... kray-k chool-a [kolly]	Rocky Woodside

55 Lochgilphead
62 North Kintyre
68 South Kintyre

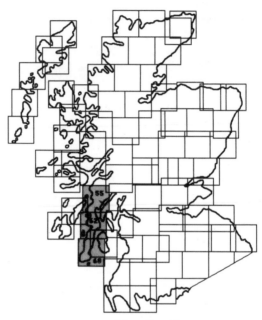

© Crown Copyright

55 LOCHGILPHEAD

Height	Mountain	Translation
526m 1726ft	**Beinn Bhreac** .... bay-n vrechk [ben vreck]	Speckled Hill
515m 1689ft	**Beinn Chapuill** .... bay-n [ben] cha-fool	Horse Hill
514m 1686ft	**An Suidhe** .... an soo-ya	The Sitting
491m 1610ft	**Carn Duchra** .... karn dooch-ra	Heritage Hill
482m 1581ft	**Beinn Dearg** .... bay-n [ben] jer-ak	Red Hill
470m 1542ft	**Creachan Dubh** .... krech-an doo	The Black Clam
466m 1528ft	**Cruach Lusach** .... kroo-ach loos-ach	Stack of Herbs

Height	Mountain	Translation
459m 1506ft	**Beinn Dubh Airigh** .... bay-n [ben] doo arry	Hill of the Black Pasture
458m 1502ft	**Cruach nan Caorach** .... kroo-ach nan kou-rach	Rocky Stack of the Sheep
438m 1437ft	**Beinn Laoigh** .... bay-n [ben] lou-ch	Calf Hill
438m 1437ft	**Carn Dearg**....................... karn jer-ak	Red Hill
420m 1378ft	**Beinn Ghlas** .... bay-n [ben] glas	Green Hill
419m 1374ft	**Cruach na h-Eanchainn** ... kroo-ach na hen-chin	Rocky Stack of Audacity
380m 1246ft	**Cruach na Seilcheig** .... kroo-ach na shel-cheg	Rocky Stack of the Snails
378m 1240ft	**Cruach Maolachy**............. kroo-ach moul-achy	Blunt Rock Stack
373m 1223ft	**Cruach Narrachan**............ kroo-ach nar-ach-acn	Fierce Rock Stack
360m 1181ft	**Dun Leacainn**................... doon [dun] lech-tan	Sloping Slab Fort
360m 1181ft	**Cruach Breacain** .... kroo-ach breck-an	Rocky Stack of the Plaid
339m 1120ft	**Meall Ruadh** .... me-yal roo-ah	Red Hill
332m 1089ft	**Cruach nam Fearna** .... kroo-ach nam feer-na	Rocky Stack of the Alder Trees
319m 1046ft	**Beinn Bhan** .... bay-n [ben] van	White Hill
314m 1030ft	**Cnoc nam Broighleag** ...... krok nam broy-lak	Hillock of the Whortleberry
303m 994ft	**Tom an t-Saighdeir**.......... toam an tay-jir [tom an say-jir]	Mound of the Soldier
301m 987ft	**Dun Dubh** .... doon [dun] doo	Black Fort
296m 971ft	**Cruach na Seilcheig** .... kroo-ach na shel-cheg	Rocky Stack of the Snails
281m 922ft	**Creag a'Chapuill**.............. kray-k a cha-fool	Horse Rock
265m 869ft	**Cnoc Reamhar** .... krok ra-var	Fat Hillock
234m 767ft	**Creag Madaidh Beag**....... kray-k ma-tay bay-k [beg]	Rock of the Small Fox
233m 764ft	**Cruach an Earbaige** .... kroo-ach an erp-ak	Rocky Stack of the Roe-Deer
174m 501ft	**Barr nan Damh** .... bar nan dav	Summit of the Stag

62 NORTH KINTYRE

Height	Mountain	Translation
562m 1843ft	**Beinn Tarsuinn** .... bay-n [ben] tar-sin	Transverse Hill
477m 1565ft	**Cruach a'Phubuill** .... kroo-ach a foo-bill	Rocky Stack of the Tent
422m 1384ft	**Cnoc a'Bhaille-Shios** .... krok a val-la shees	Hillock of the Downward Farm
364m 1194ft	**Cruach Mhic an t'Saoir** .... kroo-ach vik an tour [shou-ir]	Rocky Stack of Redemption
294m 964ft	**Cnoc Glas** .... krock glas	Green Hillock
270m 886ft	**Fuar Larach** .... foor lar-ach	Cold Ruin
266m 872ft	**Creag Mhor** .... kray-k voar	Big Rock
264m 866ft	**Cnoc an t-Samhlaidh** .... krok an tav-lay [sav-lay]	Hillock of the Proverb
207m 679ft	**Cnoc na Carraige** .... krok na kar-ig	Rocky Hillock
179m 587ft	**Garadh Liath** .... gar-ah lee-ah	Grey Copse

GIGHA

100m 328ft	**Creag Bhan** .... kray-k van	White Hill

68 SOUTH KINTYRE

454m 1489ft	**Beinn an Tuirc** .... bay-n [ben] toork	Hill of the Boar
446m 1463ft	**Cnoc Moy** .... krok moy	unknown
428m 1403ft	**Beinn na Lice** .... bay-n [ben] na leeka	unknown
408m 1338ft	**Bord Mor** .... boort more	Big Table
397m 1302ft	**Sgreadan Hill** .... skree-tan hill	Screeching Hill
352m 1155ft	**Beinn Ghuileann** .... bay-n [ben] chool-yan	Weeping Hill
330m 1082ft	**Cnoc Reamhar** .... krok ra-var	Fat Hillock
277m 909ft	**Cnoc Odhar** .... krok oh-er	Dappled Hill

56 Inveraray and Loch Lomond
(11 Munros)
(10 Corbetts)

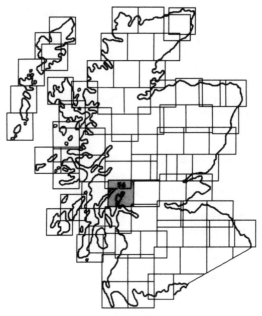

© Crown Copyright

56 INVERARAY AND LOCH LOMOND

Height	Mountain	Translation	Map Ref.
❏ **1046m**	**Cruach Ardrain**.................	Stack of the High Peak	409212
3431ft	kroo-ach ar-dran		
❏ **1011m**	**Ben Ime**	Butter Mountain	255085
3316ft	ben eem		
❏ **995m**	**An Caisteal**	The Castle.........................	379193
3264ft	an kash-t-yal		
❏ **974m**	**Ben Lomond**	Beacon Mountain	367029
3195ft	ben loam-and		
❏ **948m**	**Beinn Bhuidhe**	Yellow Mountain...............	204187
3109ft	bay-n voo-ya [ben boo-ee]		
❏ **946m**	**Ben Tulaichean**................	Mountain of the Hillocks...	416196
3104ft	ben tool-ach-an		
❏ **943m**	**Ben Vorlich**	Mountain of the Bay	295123
3094ft	ben vor-leech		
❏ **940m**	**Beinn A'Chroin**	Mountain of Danger..........	394186
3084ft	bay-n [ben] a chroy-n		

Height	Mountain	Translation	Map Ref.
❏ 933m 3067ft	**Beinn Chabhair** bay-n [ben] cha-var	Hawk Mountain	367180
❏ 926m 3038ft	**Ben Narnain** ben nar-nay-n	unknown	272067
❏ 915m 3002ft	**Ben Vane** ben vane	Middle Mountain	278098
○ 901m 2955ft	**Ben a Lochain** ben an loch-in	Hill of the Small Loch	218079
885m 2903ft	**Ben Chorranach** ben chor-ran-ach	Hill of the Lament	
○ 881m 2890ft	**The Cobbler** or **Ben Arthur**	The Shoemaker	259058
○ 865m 2837ft	**Stob a'Choin** stop a choy-n	Peak of the Dog	416161
○ 857m 2811ft	**Beinn Luibhean** bay-n [ben] loo-ven	Hill of the Plant	243079
849m 2785ft	**A'Chrois** a chrosh	The Cross	
○ 847m 2778ft	**Ben Donnich** ben don-neech	Brownish Hill	218043
815m 2673ft	**Stob Glas** stop glas	Green Peak	
814m 2670ft	**Meall Dhamh** me-yal dav	Hill of the Stags	
○ 811m 2660ft	**Beinn An Fhidhleir** bay-n [ben] an fee-ler	Fiddler's Hill	230109
803m 2634ft	**Cean Garbh** k-yan garv	Rugged Head	
○ 787m 2581ft	**The Brack** the brak	Speckled Hill	246031
○ 779m 2555ft	**Ben Bheula** ben ve-oola	Hill of the Opening	155983
○ 769m 2522ft	**Beinn a'Choin** bayn [ben] a choy-n	Hill of the Dog	354130
○ 764m 2506ft	**Meall an Fhudair** me-yal an foo-dir	Gunpowder Hill	271192
761m 2496ft	**Cnoc Connich** krok kon-yeech	Mossy Mound	
747m 2450ft	**Meall Mor** me-yal more	Big Hill	
741m 2430ft	**Beinn Mhor** bay-n [ben] voar	Big Hill	
734m 2408ft	**Doune Hill** doon hill	Fort Hill	
734m 2408ft	**Troisgeach** troshk-yach	Hill of Hunger	

Height	Mountain	Translation
732m 2401ft	**Stob an'Eas**...................... stop an es	Peak of the Waterfall
731m 2398ft	**Ptarmigan**......................... tar-mi-kan	Ptarmigan
727m 2385ft	**Stob an Bhuidhe** .... stop an voo-ya [voo-ee]	Yellow Hill
722m 2368ft	**Meall na Caora** .... me-yal na kou-ra	Hill of the Sheep
719m 2358ft	**Beinn an t'Seilich**............ bay-n [ben] an teel-eech [sheel-eech]	Hill of the Water Monster
715m 2345ft	**An Garabh**......................... an garv	Rough Hill
713m 2339ft	**Beinn Chaorach** .... bay-n [ben] chou-rach	Hill of the Sheep
708m 2322ft	**Ben Glas** .... ben glas	Green Hill
708m 2322ft	**Sron Gharbh**..................... srawn garv	Rough Point
703m 2305ft	**Beinn Lochain**................... bay-n [ben] loch-in	Hill of the Little Loch
702m 2303ft	**Beinn Eich**........................ bay-n [ben] ech	Hill of the Horses
694m 2276ft	**Beinn an t'Sidhein**........... bay-n an t-ye-en [ben an shee-yen]	Hill of Flowers
686m 2250ft	**Maol Mor** .... moul more	Big Bare Hill
684m 2244ft	**Cruach an t'Sidhein**......... kroo-ach an t-ye-en [shee-yen]	Rocky Stack of Flowers
683m 2240ft	**Beinn Damhaian**.............. bay-n [ben] dav-yan	Hill of the Stag Rut
681m 2234ft	**Beinn Bhreac** .... bay-n vrechk [ben vreck]	Speckled Hill
676m 2217ft	**Beinn Chas** .... bay-n [ben] chas	Sleepy Hill
664m 2178ft	**Beinn Ruadh** .... bay-n [ben] roo-ah	Red Hill
661m 2168ft	**Sgurr a Choinnich**............ skoor a chon-yeech	Peak of the Moss
658m 2158ft	**Stob na Boine Druim-Fhinn** stop na boy-na droom [drim] feen	Dropped Peak of the White Ridge
658m 2158ft	**Clachan Hill** .... klach-an hill	Hill of Stones
657m 2155ft	**Creachan Mor** .... kray-chan more	Big Summit
655m 2148ft	**Coire na h'Eanachan** .... cora [korry] na hay-nach-an	Hollow of the Little Marsh

Height	Mountain	Translation
655m 2148ft	**Beinn Tharsuinn** .... bay-n [ben] tar-sinn	Transverse Hill
653m 2142ft	**Stob an Fhainne** .... stop an fay-na	Ringed Peak
653m 2142ft	**Beinn Reithe** .... bay-n [ben] ree-ha	Hill of the Rams
645m 2116ft	**Maol Breac** .... moul brechk [breck]	Bare Speckled Hill
643m 2109ft	**Clach Bheinn** .... klach vay-n [ven]	Stone Hill
643m 2109ft	**Beinn Dubh** .... bay-n [ben] doo	Black Hill
641m 2102ft	**Creag Tharsuin** .... kray-k tar-sinn	Rocky Transverse
639m 2096ft	**Mullach Coire a'Chuir** .... mool-lach cora [korry] a choor	Summit of the Snow Hollow
638m 2093ft	**Balcknock** .... balk-nok	The Landmark
635m 2083ft	**Cruach a'Bhuic** . ... kroo-ach a voo-ik	Stack of the Roe Deer
634m 2080ft	**Carnach Mor** .... karn-ach more	Big Rocky Hill
633m 2076ft	**Cruinn a'Bheinn** .... kroon a vay-n [ven]	Round Hill
632m 2073ft	**Tullich Hill** .... tool-leech hill	Hillock Hill
623m 2043ft	**Beinn Breac** .... bay-n brechk [ben breck]	Speckled Hill
621m 2037ft	**Beinn Tharsuinn** .... bay-n [ben] tar-sinn	Transverse Hill
621m 2037ft	**Stob Glas** .... stop glas	Green Hill
618m 2027ft	**Beinn Bheag** .... bay-n vay-k [ben beg]	Little Hill
613m 2010ft	**Stob nan Eighrach** .... stop nan ay-rach	Peak of the Cloudberries
610m 2001ft	**Cruach nam Mult** .... kroo-ach nam moolt	Rocky Stack of the Young Sheep

57 Stirling and The Trossachs
(3 Munros)
(5 Corbetts)

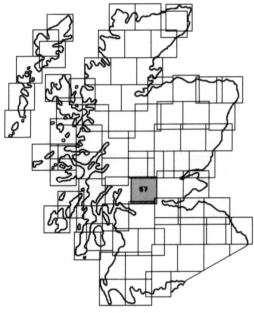

© Crown Copyright

57 STIRLING AND THE TROSSACHS

Height	Mountain	Translation	Map Ref.
❑ 1165m 3821ft	**Stob Binnein** stop bin-yan	Pinnacle Peak	435227
❑ 985m 3232ft	**Ben Vorlich** ben vor-leech	Mountain of the Bay	629189
❑ 975m 3199ft	**Stuc a'Chroin** stook a chroy-n	Peak of Danger	617175
○ 879m 2884ft	**Ben Ledi** ben leddy	God's Hill	562098
○ 820m 2690ft	**Ben Vane** ben vane	White Hill	535137
○ 813m 2667ft	**Beinn Each** bay-n [ben] yach	Hill of the Horse	602158
○ 809m 2654ft	**Meall na Fearna** me-yal na feer-na	Hill of the Alder Trees	651186
○ 771m 2529ft	**Stob Fear-Tomhais** stop fay-r to-vash	Surveyor's Peak	474163

Height	Mountain	Translation
742m 2434ft	**Coire na Cloiche** .... cora [korry] na kloy-ch	Hollow of the Stones
739m 2424ft	**Beinn Domhnuill** .... bay-n [ben] doo-ool	Donald's Hill
729m 2392ft	**Ben Venue** .... ben ven-oo	Hill of the Caves
715m 2345ft	**Ardandave** .... ard-an-dav	Heights of the Stags
715m 2345ft	**Taobh na Coille** .... touv na koola [kolly]	The Wood Side
703m 2306ft	**Beinn Bhreac** .... bay-n vrechk [ben vreck]	Speckled Hill
697m 2286ft	**Creag nan Sgiath** .... kray-k nan skee-ah	Rock of the Wings
687m 2253ft	**Beinn Bhreac** .... bay-n vrechk [ben vreck]	Speckled Hill
686m 2250ft	**Stob Breac** .... stop brechk [breck]	Speckled Peak
678m 2224ft	**Meall Reamhar** .... me-yal ra-var	Hill of the Fat Lump
674m 2211ft	**Moine nan Each** .... mawn nan yach	Peat Bog of the Horse
669m 2194ft	**An Stuchd** .... an stooch-t	The Stack
665m 2182ft	**Uamh Bheag** .... oo-av vay-k [beg]	Small Cave
662m 2172ft	**Stuc Dhubh** .... stook doo	Black Peak
657m 2155ft	**Creag Mhor** .... kray-k voar	Big Rock
653m 2141ft	**Cnoc Odhar** .... krok oh-er	Dappled Hill
647m 2122ft	**Meall Monachvie** .... me-yal mon-ach-i	Moorland Hill
646m 2119ft	**Meall Odhar** .... me-yal oh-er	Dappled Hill
640m 2099ft	**Mor Bheinn** .... more vay-n [ven]	Big Hill
634m 2080	**Stuc Odhar** .... stook oh-er	Dappled Stack
632m 2073ft	**Beinn Odhar** .... bayn [ben] oh-er	Dappled Hill
626m 2053ft	**Creag nan Speireag** .... kray-k nan speer-ay-k	Hill of the Sparrow Hawk
616m 2020ft	**Beinn an Fhogharaidh** ..... bay-n [ben] an fooch-ar-ay	Hill of the Exile

60 Islay
61 Jura and Colonsay
(1 Corbett)

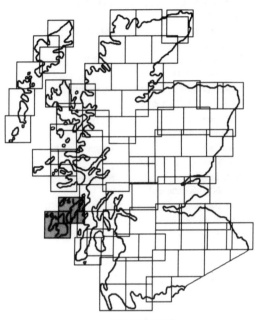

© Crown Copyright

60 ISLAY

Height	Mountain	Translation
491m 1610ft	**Beinn Bheigheir**............... bay-n [ben] veech-ir	Hill of the Beaker
472m 1548ft	**Glas Bheinn**...................... glas vay-n [ven]	Green Hill
472m 1548ft	**Beinn Bhan**....................... bay-n van [ben]	White Hill
454m 1489ft	**Beinn Uraraidh**............... bay-n [ben] oor-ay	Hill of the Monster
429m 1407ft	**Sgorr na Faoilean**............ skoor na foul-an	Peak of the Seagull
364m 1194ft	**Sgarbh Breac**................... skarv brechk [breck]	Speckled Cormorant
347m 1120ft	**Beinn Sholum**.................. bay-n [ben] shool-oom	Hill of Abundance

Height	Mountain	Translation	Map Ref.
337m 1105ft	**Beinn Caillich** .... bay-n [ben] kal-yeech	Old Woman's Hill	
316m 1036ft	**Giur Bheinn**...................... gee-oor vay-n [ven]	Goose Hill	
294m 964ft	**Sgarbh Dhubh**................. skar doo	Black Wing	
286m 938m	**Beinn Breac** .... bay-n brechk [ben breck]	Speckled Hill	
267m 876ft	**Beinn Dubh** .... bay-n [ben] doo	Black Hill	
232m 761ft	**Beinn Tart a'Mhill** .... bay-n [ben] tarsh-t a vill	Hill of the Rough Mound	
202m 662ft	**Beinn Mor** .... bay-n [ben] more	Big Hill	
182m 597ft	**Cnoc Donn** .... krok dawn	Brown Hillock	
165m 541ft	**Maol Buidhe** .... moul boo-ya [boo-ee]	Yellow Bare Hill	
128m 420ft	**Cnoc Uamh nan Feur**....... krok oo-av nan fee-ar	Hillock of the Grassy Cave	

GIGHA

100m 328ft	**Creag Bhan** .... kray-k van	White Rock	

61 JURA AND COLONSAY

JURA

○ **785m** 2578ft	**Beinn an Oir**.................... bay-n [ben] an or	Hill of the Border* or Gold	498749
755m 2476ft	**Beinn Shiantaidh** .... bay-n [ben] she-an-tay	Holy Hill*	
734m 2407ft	**Beinn a'Chaolais** .... bay-n [ben] a choul-ash	Hill of the Narrows*	

* Known as the Paps [breasts] of Jura.

575m 1886ft	**Corra Bheinn**.................... cora vay-n [ven]	Peaked Hill	
561m 1840ft	**Glas Bheinn** .... glas vayn [ven]	Green Hill	
530m 1738ft	**Dubh Bheinn** .... doo vay-n [ven]	Black Hill	

Height	Mountain	Translation
508m 1666ft	**Scrindale** .... skrin-dale	Scree Valley
477m 1565ft	**Dhubh Bheinn** .... doo vayn [ven]	Black Hill
467m 1532ft	**Beinn Bhreac** .... bay-n vrechk [ben vreck]	Speckled Hill
453m 1486ft	**Rainberg** .... rain-berg	unknown
438m 1437ft	**Beinn Bhreac** .... bay-n vrechk [ben vreck]	Speckled Hill
365m 1197ft	**Ben Garrisdale**................. ben gar-ris-dale	unknown
342m 1122ft	**Brat Bheinn** .... brat vay-n [ven]	Apron Hill
337m 1105ft	**Cruach an Uillt Fhearna** .. kroo-ach an oo-lt feer-na	Stack of the Oily Man
319m 1046ft	**Cruib** .... kroob	The Bend
296m 971ft	**Cruach na Seilcheig** .... kroo-ach na shel-cheg	Rocky Stack of the Snails
295m 968ft	**Cruach Ionnastail** .... kroo-ach yon-ash-tal	Rocky Stack of the Treasure
190m 623ft	**Beinn Sgaillinish**............. bay-n [ben] skal-e-nish	Shady Hill
175m 574ft	**Staon Bheinn** .... stoun ven	Hill of the Juniper Tree
175m 574ft	**Na h-Ursainnan** .... na hoor-san-an	The Pillars

COLONSAY

Height	Mountain	Translation
143m 469ft	**Carnan Eoin** .... karn-an yon	Ian's Cairn
139m 456ft	**Beinn Bhreac** .... bay-n vrechk [ben vreck]	Speckled Hill
135m 443ft	**Carn Mor**.......................... karn more	Big Hill
113m 436ft	**Beinn nan Caorach** .... bay-n [ben] nan kou-rach	Hill of the Sheep
120m 394ft	**Binnein Riabhach** .... bin-yan ree-vach	Grizzled Peak

63 Firth of Clyde
69 Isle of Arran
(4 Corbetts)

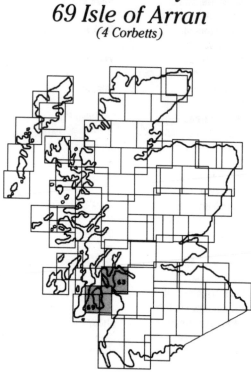

© Crown Copyright

63 FIRTH OF CLYDE

COWAL PENINSULA

578m 1896ft	**Cruach nan Caorach** .... kroo-ach nan kou-rach	Rocky Stack of the Sheep
568m 1863ft	**Leacann nan Gall** .... l-ye-ch-tan nan gawl	Sloping Hill of the Lowlander
498m 1633ft	**Cruach na Maoile** .... kroo-ach na moula	Bare Rocky Stack
473m 1551ft	**Blar Buidhe** .... blaar boo-ya [boo-ee]	Yellow Hill of the Plain
418m 1371ft	**Corlaraich** .... kor-lar-ach	Hill of Excess
378m 1240ft	**Sron Dearg** .... srawn jer-ak	Red Point
346m 1135ft	**Buachailean** .... booch-al-yan	The Herdsman

Height	Mountain	Translation	Map Ref.

322m **Beinn Ruadha** .... Red Hill
1056ft bay-n [ben] roo-ah

313m **Cnoc a'Mhadaidh**............ Hillock of the Fox
1027ft krok a va-tay

292m **Meall Buidhe** .... Yellow Hill
958ft me-yal boo-ya [boo-ee]

209m **Tom Odhar** .... Dappled Hill
686ft toam [tom] oh-er

NORTH-WEST MAINLAND

506m **Beinn Breac** .... Speckled Hill
1660ft bay-n [ben] bre-cht

497m **Stuchdan**.......................... The Stacks
1630ft stooch-tan

484m **Meallan Riabhach** .... Grizzled Hill
1588ft me-yal-an ree-vach

465m **Dun Mor**........................... Big Fort
1525ft doon more

449m **Sgian Dubh** .... Black Knife
1473ft skee-an doo

443m **Meallan Sidhein** .... Hill of the Fairies
1453ft me-yal-lan she-yen

393m **Creag nan Fitheach** .... Rocky Cliff of the Ravens
1289ft kray-k nan fee-ach

303m **Cnoc Breamanach** .... Hillock of the Tail
994ft krok brem-an-ach

294m **Toman Dubh** .... Black Mound
964ft toam-an doo

69 ISLE OF ARRAN

○ **874m** **Goat Fell** .... Goat Peak.......................... 991415
2867ft

○ **859m** **Caisteal Abhail** .... Castle Orchard.................. 969444
2818ft kash-tyal av-al

○ **826m** **Beinn Tarsuinn** .... Transverse Hill 959412
2710ft bay-n [ben] tar-sin

819m **Mullach Buidhe** .... Yellow Summit
2686ft mool-lach boo-ya [boo-ee]

810m **North Goat Fell** .... North Goat Peak
2657ft

○ **799m.** **Cir Mor**............................. Big Comb 973432
2621ft keer more

792m **Beinn Nuis** .... Milk Hill
2598ft bay-n [ben] noos

Height	Mountain	Translation
721m 2365ft	**Mullach Buidhe** .... mool-lach boo-ya [boo-ee]	Yellow Hill
715m 2345ft	**Beinn Bharrain**............... bay-n [ben] var-ran	Pointed Hill
711m 2332ft	**Beinn Bhreac** .... bay-n vrechk [ben vreck]	Speckled Hill
662m 2171m	**Am Binnein** .... am bin-yan	The Peak
661m 2168ft	**Cioch na h'Oighe** .... kee-och na hoy-ya	The Virgin's Breast
653m 2142ft	**Beinn Chliabhain**............ bay-n [ben] chlee-av-an	Hill of the Basket
634m 2080ft	**Suidhe Fhearghas** .... soo-ya fer-gas	Sitting Fergus
573m 1879ft	**Beinn Bhreac** .... bayn vrechk [ben vreck]	Speckled Hill
570m 1870ft	**Meall nan Damh** .... me-yal nan dav	Hill of the Deer
549m 1801ft	**Meall Donn** .... me-yal dawn	Brown Hill
523m 1715ft	**Beinn Tarsuinn** .... bay-n [benj tar-sin	Transverse Hill
512m 1679ft	**A'Chruach** .... a chroo-ach	The Stack
512m 1679ft	**Ard Bheinn**...................... ard vay-n [ven]	High Hill
503m 1650ft	**Beinn Bhreac** .... ben vrechk [ben vreck]	Speckled Hill
491m 1610ft	**Meall Mor** .... me-yal more	Big Hill
479m 1571ft	**Sail Chalmadale**.............. saal chal-ma-dale	Heel of Hjalmund's Glen
479m 1571ft	**Beinn Bhiorach** .... bay-n [ben] vee-rach	Sharp Hill
458m 1502ft	**Tighvein**........................... ti-ven	Big House
444m 1456ft	**Fionn Bhealach**................ fee-on v-yal-ach	White Pass
435m 1427ft	**Meall Bhig** .... me-yal vik	Chirping Hill
417m 1368ft	**Cnoc a'Chapuill** .... krok a cha-fool	Hill of the Horse
409m 1342ft	**Creag Ghlas Laggan**........ kray-k chlas lag-gan	Little Green Hollow
406m 1332ft	**Brisderg** .... brees-jerk	Broken Place of the Red Deer

Height	Mountain	Translation
406m 1332ft	**Sguiler** .... skooler	The Basket
373m. 1223ft	**Sheans** .... sheens	Fairy Hill
362m 1187ft	**Cnoc Breac Gamhainn** ..... krok brechk [breck] gavan	Hill of the Speckled Calf
361m 1184ft	**An Tunna** .... an toon-na	The Cask
353m 1158ft	**Cnoc na Dail** .... krok na dal	The Field Hillock
337m 1105ft	**Scrivan** .... skree-van	White Scree
309m 1013ft	**Clachan** .... klach-an	Stone House
301m 987ft	**The Ross**	Wooded Promontory
295m 968ft	**Innis Dubh** .... een-ish doo	Black Meadow
294m 964ft	**Beinn Tarsuinn** .... bay-n [ben] tar-sin	Transverse Hill
280m 918ft	**Beinn Chaorach** .... bay-n [ben] chou-rach	Hill of the Sheep
272m 892ft	**Cnoc Nan Sgrath** .... krok nan skra	Hillock of the Skin
228m 748ft	**Beinn Lochain** .... bay-n [ben] loch-in	Hill of the Little Loch

HOLY ISLE

Height	Mountain	Translation
314m 1030ft	**Mullach Mor** .... mool-lach more	Big Summit

5. REFERENCE SECTION

Mountain Components

In the interests of brevity, this guide does not contain translations for all the upland features shown on OS maps. The list below includes most of the Gaelic words used to descibe high ground in Scotland. Use these components and translate for yourself the names of hill, peaks and crags not listed in the guide.

Note: The spellings listed below are as you would find in a modern Gaelic dictionary. You may find that they may differ from the spellings used on maps – some words may contain extra vowels or consonants (particularly h) or both.

a or *an* translates as *the*; *nan* or *nam* translates as *of the*

A

abhainn	av-in	river
achadh	ach-ah	field
aighean	ay-yan	deer
airgiod	er-e-kit	silver
airidh	arry	pasture
allt	all-t	stream
aodann	ou-tan	face
aonach	ou-nach	ridge/hill
	[an-ach]	or moor
aosda	ou-sta	old
ard	ard	high

B

bac	bak	bank
bad	bad	tuft/cluster
ban	ban	white
barr	barr	summit
beag	bay-k	little
	[beg]	
bealach	b-yal-ach	mountain pass/gorge
beinn	bay-n	mountain/hill

beithe	bee	birch tree
ben	ben	mountain/hill
beul	bi-al	mouth
bidean	beet-yan	peak
binnein	bin-yan	peak
blar	blaar	plain
bo	bo	cow
bodach	botach	old man
boidheach	boy-yach	beautiful
bradan	bra-tan	salmon
braigh	bray	slope
breac	brechk [breck]	speckled
bruach	broo-ach	earth bank
buidhe	boo-ya [boo-ee]	yellow

C

caber	ka-ber	stag's antler
cac	kach	dirty
cailleach	kal-yach	old woman
cairn	kayr-n	pile of stones
caisteal	kash-t-yal	castle
calpa	kalpa	nail
cam	kam	crooked
caol	koul	narrow
caora	kou-ra	sheep
caorach	kou-rach	sheep
caorann	kou-ran	rowan tree
carn	karn	rocky hill or mountain
cas	kash	steep
ceann	k-yann	head
cearc	k-yark	hen
ceo	k-yo	mist
chapuill	cha-fool	horses
choin	choy-n	dog
ciche	keesh-ta	breast
cioch	kee-ach	breast
cir	keer	comb
ciste	kee-sta	chest
clach	klach	stone
clachan	klach-an	stone dwelling
cleireach	kler-ach	clergyman
cloich	kloy-ch	stone
cnap	krap	lump
cnoc	krok	hillock
coileach	kil-yach	cockerel
coille	kool-a [kolly]	woodland
coinneach	kon-yach	moss/bog

coinnich	kon-yeech	moss/meeting
coire	cora	mountain hollow/
	[korry]	bowl shaped
craobh	kroov	tree
creag	kray-k	rock/cliff
crioch	kree-och	boundary
crodh	kro	cattle
crois	krosh	cross
croit	krawt	croft
crom	krom	crooked
cruach	kroo-ach	rock stack
cruib	kroob	bend
cul	kool	back/ridge

D

damh	dav	deer/stag
dearg	jer-ak	red
deas	jes	south
diollaid	jeel-at	saddle
doire	dor-ee	thicket
	[dora]	
donn	dawn	brown
drochaid	droch-at	bridge
druim	droom	ridge
	[drim]	
dubh	doo	black
dun	doon	fort
	[dun]	

E

each	yach	horse
eag	ayk	notch
eagach	ay-kach	notched
eaglais	eg-lish	church
ear	er	east
earb	erb	roe deer
eas	es	waterfall
eich	ech	horses
eilean	eel-an	island
eilid	eelj	deer (hind)
elrig	el-rik	deer trap
eoin	yawn	birds
eun	ayn	bird

F

fada	fata	long
falt	faw-lt	hair
fas	fas	empty
fasgach	fas-kach	sheltered
fear	fay-r	man
feith	fee	bog

feur	fer	grass
fiacal	fee-kil	tooth
fiadh	fee	deer
fion	fin	wine
fionn	fee-on	fair/white
fluich	flooch	wet
fraoch	frouch	heather
frith	free	deer forest
fuar	foor	cold
fuaran	foor-an	well

G

gall	gawl	lowlander
gaoith	gou	windy
gaorr	gour	dirty
garabh	gar-ah	garden
garbh	garv	rough
geal	g-yal	white
gille	gilly	young man
giubhais	goo-vash	pine tree
glas	glas	grey/green
gobhal	gow-al	fork
gobhar	gour	goat
gorm	gor-om	blue
grian	gree-an	sun
gruamach	groo-mach	gloomy

I

iar	ear	west
iarunn	ear-oon	iron
im	eem	butter
innis	een-ish	meadow/island
iolair	yool-ir	eagle
isean	ish-an	young bird
iubhar	yoo-var	yew tree

L

labhar	la-var	loud
lag	lag	hollow
lairig	lar-ig	pass/glen
laogh	lou-ch	calf
larach	lar-ach	ruin
leac	l-y-echt [le-cht]	rock slab
leana	lee-ana	meadow
leathad	lay-hat	meadow
leith	lay	half
leum	lee-om	leap
liath	lee-ah	grey
linnie	l-yeena	pool
loin	loy-n	glade

lom	low-m	bare
lon	low-n	meadow/marsh
lub	loop	bend
lurg	loor-k	stem
lus	loos	herb/plant

M

mac	mak	son
machair	ma-chir	sandy field
madadh	ma-tay	fox/dog
maighdean	may-yan	maiden
mam	mam	breast/round hill
maol	moul	bare
marbh	mar-av	dead
mathair	ma-hir	mother
meadhon	mee-yon	middle
meall	me-yal	hill/lump
mhurlaig	voor-lak	bay
mil	meel	honey
moine	moy-n	peat
monadh	mon-ah	moor/mountain
mor	more	big
muc	mook	pig
muillinn	mool-lin	mill
mullach	mool-lach	ridge/summit

N

nead	net	nest
neimheis	nee-vash	venom
nuadh	noo-ah	new
nuas	noo-as	down

O

odhar	oh-er	dappled
og	awk	young
oir	or	border/gold
olk	awlk	evil
ord	aw-rd	hammer

P

pap	paap	breast
pean	pe-un	sheep pen
piob	peeb	pipe
poit	poy-t	pot
poll	pool	hole
preas	presh	bush
puist	poosht	post (fence)

R

raineach	ran-yach	fern
reamhar	ra-var	fat

riabhach	ree-vach	grizzled/greyish evil one
righ	ree	king
ros	ross	promontory
ruadh	roo-ah	red

S

sabhal	sav-al	barn
sagairt	sa-gart	priest
sail	saal	heel
seilch	shel-ch	monster
sgian	skee-an	knife
sgiath	skee-ah	wing
sgor	skoor	peak
sgriob	skreeb	scrape
sgul	skool	shelter
sgurr	skoor	peak
sian	she-an	storm
sionnach	shoon-ach	fox's den
sithean	she-hen	fairy hillock
sloc	slok	pit
slugan	slook-an	swallowing
snechda	sh-nech-ta	snow
socach	soch-ach	beak
srath	srah	glen
sron	srawn	point/nose
stac	stak	peak
starbh	starv	stout
stob	stop	peak
stri	stree	strife
stuc	stook	stack
suas	soos	upper

T

talamh	tal-ac	earth
tana	ta-na	thin
taobh	touv	side
tarsuinn	tar-sin	transverse/ crossing
teanga	t-yen-ga	tongue
tigh	ti	house
tioram	tee-ram	dry
tir	t-yeer	land
toll	toll	hole
tom	toam [tom]	round hill/ mound
tri	tree	three
tuath	too-ah	north
tulach	tool-ach	hillock
tur	toor	tower

171

U

uaine	oo-ayn	green
uamh	oo-av	cave
uan	oo-an	lamb
uchd	ooch-t	point
uiseag	oosh-ak	lark
uisge	oosh-ki	water
ur	oor	new

Scottish Place Name Pronunciation Guide

A

Aberchirder	a-ber-kir-der
Achnasheen	ach-na-sheen
Achnashellach	ach-na-she-lach
Achnult	ach-nul-t
Alloa	al-o-wa
Alloway	al-o-way
Altnabrec	alt-na-breck
Alves	al-vis
Amulree	aml-ree
Ardcharnich	ard-kar-nich
Ardersier	ard-der-seer
Ardgour	ard-gour
Ardlui	ard-loo-i
Ardnamurchan	ard-na-murk-an
Ardrishaig	ar-drish-aig
Ardrossan	ar-draw-sun
Ardvasar	ard-vaz-ar
Arisaig	ar-is-aig
Arrochar	ar-och-ar
Ascog	as-kog
Assynt	ass-int
Atholl	a-thol
Auchenblae	awch-en-blay
Auchterardar	awch-ter-ard-ar
Auchtermuchty	awch-ter-much-ty
Aultbea	awlt-bay
Aviemore	av-i-more
Aultguish	awlt-goo-ish
Aylth	ail-th

B

Balbeggie	bal-beg-gi
Balfour	bal-fur

Ballachulish	bal-a-hool-ish
Ballantrae	bal-an-tray
Ballater	bal-a-ter
Ballinluig	bal-in-loo-ig
Balmacara	bal-ma-ka-ra
Balmaha	bal-ma-ha
Balmoral	bal-maw-ral
Balnacra	bal-na-kra
Balquhidder	bal-whid-der
Banavie	ban-av-i
Banchory	banch-or-i
Banff	bamf
Bannockburn	ban-nock-burn
Beasdale	bees-dale
Beauly	b-you-li
Bellochantuy	bell-och-anti
Benbecula	ben-beck-u-la
Blair Athol	blayr a-thol
Boat of Garten	boat of gar-ten
Borthwick	borth-wick
Bracadale	brak-a-dale
Braco	bra-ko
Braemore	bray-more
Breadalbane	bred-al-ban
Bridge of Balgie	bridge of bal-gi
Bridge of Orchy	bridge of or-ki
Brodrick	braw-dick
Brora	bro-ra
Broughton	braw-ton
Broughty Ferry	braw-ti ferry
Bruar	brew-er
Buccleuch	buck-loo
Buchlyvie	buck-li-vi
Burntisland	burnt-yle-and

C

Caerlavorock	kar-lav-er-ock
Calvine	kal-ven
Campbeltown	kam-bel-ton
Cardenden	kar-din-den
Carnoustie	kar-noos-ti
Castlecary	ka-sel-kay-ri
Cawdor	kaw-dor
Clachaig	klach-aig
Clachnaharry	klach-na-hari
Clackmannan	klack-man-nan
Cleish	kleesh
Cluanie	kloo-ni
Colmonell	kall-mon-el
Colonsay	kol-on-say
Comrie	kum-ri

Connell	kon-el
Corrour	kor-our
Cowal	kow-al
Coylumbridge	koy-lum-bridge
Crieff	kreef
Crianlarich	kree-an-lar-ich
Crichton	kry-tun
Cromarty	krom-mer-ti
Crombie	krom-bi
Cruden Bay	kroo-den bay
Culloden	kul-aw-den
Culross	koo-rus
Cupar	koo-per

D

Dalhousie	dal-how-si
Dalnaspidal	dal-na-spi-dal
Dalrymple	dal-rim-pel
Dalwhinnie	dal-whin-i
Dalziel	dee-ell
Dechmont	dech-mont
Dores	dors
Douglas	dug-las
Doune	doon
Dounreay	doon-ray
Drumelzier	drum-el-zir
Drumnadrochit	drum-na-drawch-it
Drumochter	drum-och-ter
Dryburgh	dry-bur-a
Drymen	dri-mem
Dunbeath	dun-beeth
Dunfermline	dun-ferm-lin
Dunvegan	dun-vaig-an
Dyce	dice
Dysart	die-sart

E

Edinburgh	e-din-bur-ah
Eigg	egg
Eilan Donan	ee-lan dawn-an
Elderslie	el-der-zlee
Elgol	el-gawl
Elie	ee-li
Elphin	el-fin

F

Fenwick	fen-ik
Findon	fin-an
Fionnphort	fee-on-ort
Fochabers	fawch-a-bers
Forbes	for-bis

Fordyce	for-dice
Forres	for-res
Fowlis	fowl-is
Fraserburgh	frays-er-bur-a
Freuchie	frooch-i
Fushiebridge	foo-shi-bridge
Fyvie	fi-vi

G

Garve	garv
Georgemas	jor-ji-mas
Gigha	ge-a
Glamis	gla-mis
Glenelg	glen-el-g
Glenrothes	glen-raw-this
Glenurquhart	glen-ur-kurt
Golspie	gawl-spi
Gruinard	groo-yard

H

Halkirk	haw-kirk
Hebrides	heb-ri-dees
Helmsdale	hel-ms-dale
Hume	hewm

I

Inchnadamph	inch-na-damf
Insch	insh
Inverallochy	in-ver-al-loch-i
Inveraray	in-ver-ay-ray
Inverbervie	in-ver-ber-vi
Inverlael	in-ver-layl
Inveruglas	in-ver-oo-glas
Inverurie	in-ver-oo-ri
Iona	i-o-na
Islay	yle-a

J

Jarlshof	yarls-hof
Jura	joo-ra

K

Kames	kayms
Keith	keeth
Killiecrankie	kill-i-kran-ki
Killin	kill-in
Kilmacolm	kil-ma-comb
Kincardine	kin-kar-din
Kingussie	king-oo-si
Kinglochmoidart	kin-loch-moy-dart
Kinlocheil	kin-loch-eel

Kirkcaldy	kir-kaw-di
Kirkgunzeon	kirk-gun-yun
Kyleakin	kyle-a-kin
Kylerhea	kyle-ray
Kylesku	kyle-skew

L

Lamancha	la-man-ka
Leatham .	le-tham
Leuchars	loo-kars
Lhanbryde	lan-bride
Lochaber	loch-a-ber
Lochailort	loch-yle-ort
Locheil	loch-eel
Lochgilphead	loch-gilp-head
Lochluichart	loch-looch-art
Longformarcus	long-for-may-kus
Lossiemouth	loss-i-mouth
Loth	law-th
Luncarty	lun-car-ti
Lybster	leeb-ster

M

Machrie	mach-ri
Machrihanish	mach-ri-han-ish
Mallaig	mal-ay-g
Maryculter	mary-koo-ter
Mausdale	maws-dale
Milngavie	mill-guy
Moidart	moy-dart
Monifieth	mon-i-feeth
Moulin	mool-in

N

New Pitsligo	new pit-sly-go
Nigg	nig

P

Pennyghael	penny-gale
Peterculter	peter-kooter
Pitlochry	pit-loch-ri
Poolewe	pool-wee
Portnacroish	port-na-kroy-sh

R

Raasay	raa-say
Rhu	roo
Rum	rum
Rhynie	ri-ni
Rothes	raw-thes
Rothesay	rawth-say

Rothiemurchus .... raw-thi-mur-kus
Rowardennan.............................. row-ar-den-an
Ruthven .... riven

S
Sanquar .... san-kur
Scone .... skoon
Scourie .... scoo-ri
Skeabost .... skee-bost
Sligachan .... slee-ach-an
Snizort .... snee-zort
Strathaven .... stay-ven
Strathkanaird .... strath-kan-aird
Strathmiglo................................. strath-mig-lo
Strathyre.................................... strath-eyer
Struan.. strew-an

T
Taynuilt .... tay-nul-t
Threave .... threev
Tighnabruaich .... ti-na-broo-ach
Tiree .... tie-ree
Tobermory .... toe-ber-more-i
Tomintoul .... tawm-in-tool
Tomnavoulin................................ tawn-na-voo-lin
Tongue....................................... tung
Trossachs .... traw-sachs
Tyndrum .... tine-drum

U
Uig .... oo-ig
Uist .... you-istt
Ullapool .... ul-a-poll
Urquhart .... ur-kurt

W
Wanlockhead .... wan-lock-head
Wemyss Bay................................ weems bay

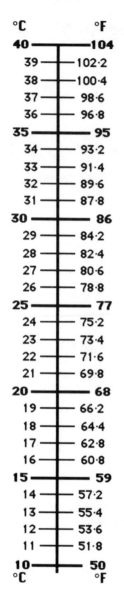

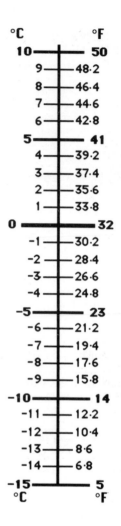

°C	°F
40	**104**
39	102·2
38	100·4
37	98·6
36	96·8
35	**95**
34	93·2
33	91·4
32	89·6
31	87·8
30	**86**
29	84·2
28	82·4
27	80·6
26	78·8
25	**77**
24	75·2
23	73·4
22	71·6
21	69·8
20	**68**
19	66·2
18	64·4
17	62·8
16	60·8
15	**59**
14	57·2
13	55·4
12	53·6
11	51·8
10	**50**
°C	°F

°C	°F
10	**50**
9	48·2
8	46·4
7	44·6
6	42·8
5	**41**
4	39·2
3	37·4
2	35·6
1	33·8
0	**32**
−1	30·2
−2	28·4
−3	26·6
−4	24·8
−5	**23**
−6	21·2
−7	19·4
−8	17·6
−9	15·8
−10	**14**
−11	12·2
−12	10·4
−13	8·6
−14	6·8
−15	**5**
°C	°F

Temperature Conversion Table
(Celsius to Fahrenheit)

Note: Temperature at 1000m (3000ft) is more than 5°C lower than at sea level.

Distance Conversion Table

Miles to Kilometers		
1m	–	1.6km
2m	–	3.2km
3m	–	4.8km
4m	–	6.4km
5m	–	8.0km
6m	–	9.6km
7m	–	11.2km
8m	–	12.8km
9m	–	14.4km
10m	–	16.0km
11m	–	17.6km
12m	–	19.2km
13m	–	20.8km
14m	–	22.4km
15m	–	24.0km
16m	–	25.6km
17m	–	27.2km
18m	–	28.8km
19m	–	30.4km
20m	–	32.0km
25m	–	40.2km
30m	–	48.2km
35m	–	56.3km
40m	–	64.2km
45m	–	72.4km
50m	–	80.4km

Kilometers to Miles		
1km	–	0.6m
2km	–	1.2m
3k m	–	1.8m
4km	–	2.5m
5km	–	3.1m
6km	–	3.7m
7km	–	4.3m
8km	–	5.0m
9km	–	5.6m
10km	–	6.2m
11km	–	6.8m
12km	–	7.6m
13km	–	8.1m
14km	–	8.7m
15km	–	9.3m
16km	–	9.9m
17km	–	10.5m
18km	–	11.1m
19km	–	11.7m
20km	–	12.4m
25km	–	15.5m
30km	–	18.6m
35km	–	21.7m
40km	–	24.8m
45km	–	27.9m
50km	–	31.0m

Walking Speeds

	Fit Person	Average	Novice
Flat Terrain (Light Pack)	6kph (3.7mph)	5kph (3.1mph)	4kph (2.5mph)
Hilly Terrain (Light Pack)	5kph (3.1mph)	4kph (2.5mph)	3kph (1.8mph)
Steep Terrain (Light Pack)	4kph (2.5mph)	3kph (1.8mph)	2kph (1.2mph)

The table above provides a *rough estimate*, of the walking speeds that can be maintained by an individual when covering routes of varying difficulty. In calculating the time needed to cover a pre-determined distance, always allow extra time for difficulties that may arise; for example, a change in overhead weather conditions, or underfoot conditions (wet ground), swollen streams and rivers, visibility, food stops and the fitness of the slowest member of your group. In addition, never simply assume the return half of your journey will be completed as quickly as the outgoing part: although you may be descending, your walking speed may drop when you are tired and hungry. If weather conditions are poor when you are about to start out, modify your plans accordingly. Remember the hills will always be there, while if you take unnecessary risks you may not.

Note. If you are using the grid on your map to calculate the distance of your journey. Remember the diagonal of the grid is approx. 1.5km, whereas the vertical and horizontal lines of the grid are 1km.

Wind Speed Chart:
Beaufort Scale

Force	Descriptive Term	MPH	KPH	KNOTS
0	CALM	0-1	0.1.5	<=1
1	LIGHT AIR	1-3	1.5-5	1-3
2	LIGHT BREEZE	4-7	6-11	4-6
3	GENTLE BREEZE	8-12	12-19	7-10
4	MODERATE BREEZE	13-18	20-29	11-16
5	FRESH BREEZE	19-24	30-39	17-21
6	STRONG BREEZE	25-31	40-50	22-27
7	NEAR GALE	32-38	51-61	28-33
8	GALE	39-46	62-74	34-40
9	STRONG GALE	47-54	75-87	41-47
10	STORM	55-63	88-101	48-55
11	VIOLENT STORM	64-72	102-116	56-63
12	HURRICANE	>=73	>=117	>=64

Note: Windspeed at 1,000 metres (3,000ft) is 2-3 times greater than at sea level.

WIND DESCRIPTION

FORCE	*0*	Smoke rises vertically.
FORCE	*1*	Smoke drifts.
FORCE	*2*	Wind felt on face, grass stirs.
FORCE	*3*	Grass sways, leaves rustle on trees.
FORCE	*4*	Clothes flutter, water ripples on lochs.
FORCE	*5*	Small tree branches sway, loose debris moves.
FORCE	*6*	Large tree branches sway, waves on lochs.
FORCE	*7*	Small trees sway, lean into wind when walking.
FORCE	*8*	Debris blown about, blown about when walking.
FORCE	*9*	Trees blown down, blown over when walking.
FORCE	*10*	Trees blown down, blown over when walking
FORCE	*11*	Buildings blown down, walking impossible.
FORCE	*12*	Buildings blown down, walking impossible.

Wind Direction

The table below summarises probable weather conditions when winds are blowing from a particular direction:

SUMMER WINDS

Direction	*Probable weather conditions*
north	cool weather especially at night, rain, fog or haze.
north-east	colder winds, but fine clear weather, possible showers on the east coast.
east	warm dry winds, clear skies, but cool and misty on the east coast.
south-east and south	hot and sunny weather, possibly thunder in the south.
south west	warm but cloudy.
west	warm and wet, hill cloud.
north-west	cool days and nights, heavy showers.

WINTER WINDS

Direction	*Probable weather conditions*
north	very cold, rain and snow.
north-east	very cold, but possible clear skies.
east	cold, rain, sleet and snow on high ground.
south-east and south	clear and cold days.
south-west	cloudy, drizzle, foggy and wet.
west	dull wet weather.
north-west	showers, frost, clear spells.

OTHER WEATHER FACTORS (VISIBILITY)

Mist	visibility 300m (1000 feet) to 50m (150 feet)
Fog	visibility below 50m (150 feet)
Dense Fog	visibility less than 15m (50 feet)

Windchill Factor

This factor should be taken into consideration on long exposed walks in winter. The Windchill Factor is calculated on the air temperature and windspeed at a given time and is issued by the Met Office in its weather forecasts. The greater the windchill the greater the danger, e.g. a temperature of -5°C + a windspeed of 40kph (25mph) at sea level gives a Windchill Factor of over -20°c (see table below). Therefore the higher you climb, the greater the danger, owing to the decreasing temperature and the increasing wind speed.

0°C to -10°C	cold
-10°C to -20°C	very cold (uncomfortable)
-20°C to -30°C	extremly cold (very uncomfortable)
-30°C to -40°C	bare skin starts to freeze (walking difficult)
-40°C to -50°C	frost bite probable on bare skin (walking dangerous)

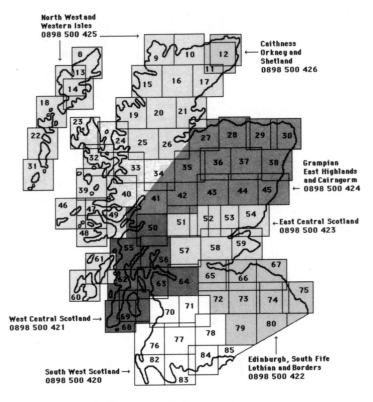

North West and
Western Isles
0898 500 425

Caithness
Orkney and
Shetland
0898 500 426

Grampian
East Highlands
and Cairngorm
0898 500 424

← East Central Scotland
0898 500 423

West Central Scotland →
0898 500 421

Edinburgh, South Fife
Lothian and Borders
0898 500 422

South West Scotland →
0898 500 420

Note: All dividing lines are approximate.

© Crown Copyright

Weather Call Map

183

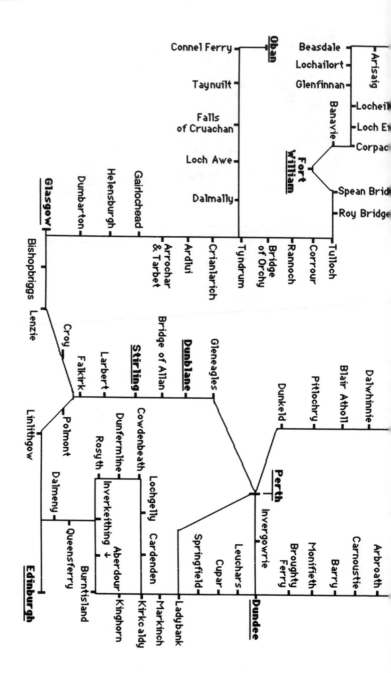

184

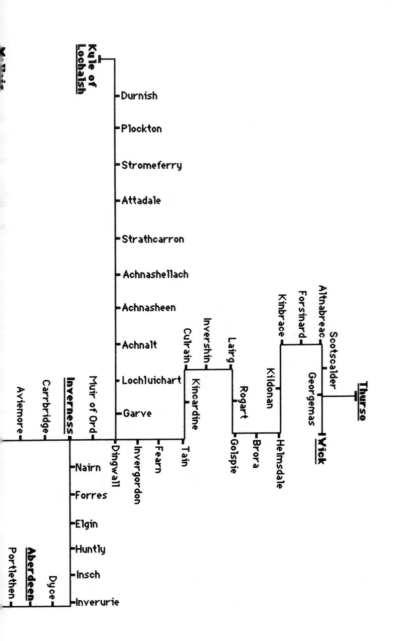

Rail Routes for Central and Northern Scotland
(Main Stations in Bold Type)

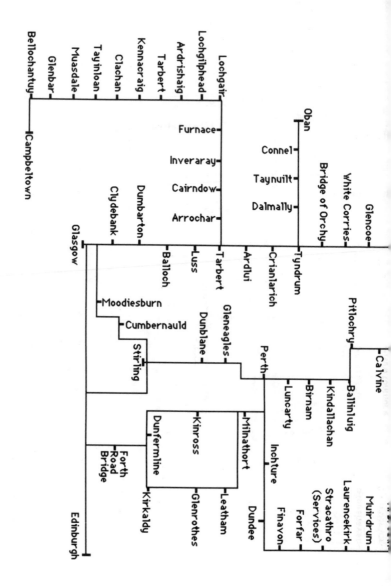

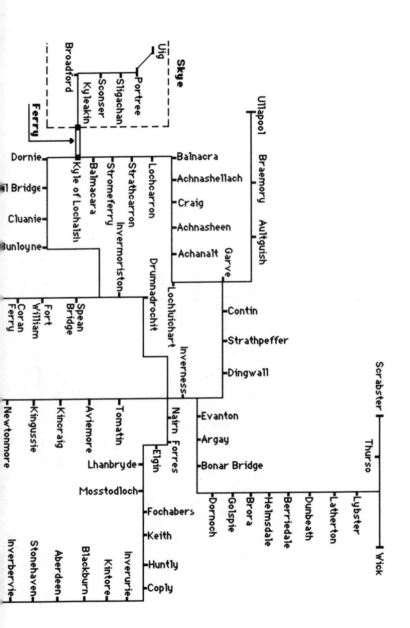

City Link Coach Routes for Central and Northern Scotland

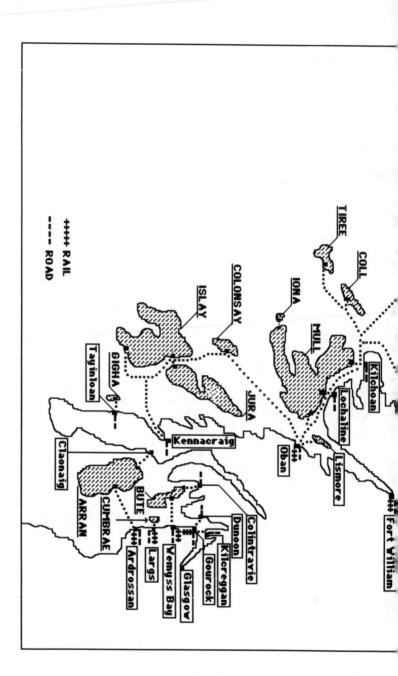

RAIL

ROAD

TIREE

COLL

COLONSAY

ISLAY

IONA

MULL

Kilchoan

Tayinloan

GIGHA

JURA

Lochaline

Lismore

Claonaig

Kennacraig

Oban

Fort William

ARRAN

CUMBRAE

BUTE

Ardrossan

Largs

Wemyss Bay

Glasgow

Gourock

Kilcreggan

Dunoon

Colintraive

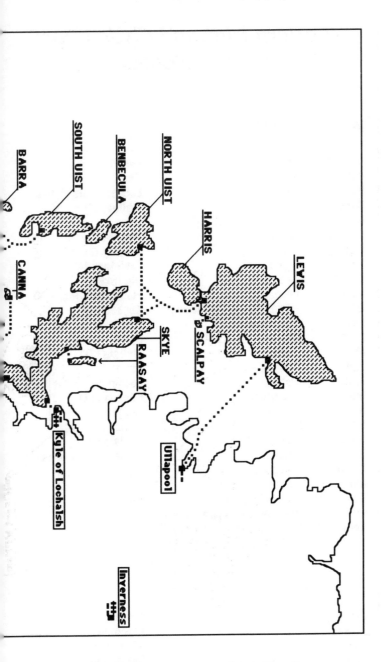

*Western Isles and Clyde Coast
Ferry Routes*

Western Isles and Clyde Coast Ferry Routes

WESTERN ISLES

Island	*Docks*	*Departs*
Barra	Castlebay	**Oban**
Barra	Castlebay	**Lochboisdale (S.Uist)**
Canna	Canna	**Mallaig (2)**
Coll	Coll via Tobermory (Mull)	**Oban**
Colonsay	Scalasaig	**Oban (4)**
Eigg	Eigg	**Mallaig (2)**
Gigha	Gigha	**Tayinloan (4)**
Harris	Tarbert	**Uig (Skye)**
Iona	Iona	**Fionnphort (Mull) (2)**
Islay	Port Ellen and Port Askaig	**Kennacraig**
Lewis	Stornoway	**Ullapool**
Lismore	Lismore	**Oban**
Muck	Muck	**Mallaig (2)**
Mull	Craignure	**Oban**
Mull	Fishnish	**Lochaline**
Mull	Tobermory	**Kilchoan (3)**
North Uist	Lochmaddy	**Uig (Skye)**
Raasay	Raasay	**Sconser (Skye)**
Rum	Rum	**Mallaig (2)**
Scalpay	Scalpay	**Kyles Scalpay (Harris)**
Skye	Armadale	**Mallaig (3)**
Skye	Kyleakin	**Kyle of Lochalsh**
South Uist	Lochboisdale	**Oban**
Tiree	Tiree via Tobermory (Mull)	**Oban**
Benbecula	There is no ferry service to this island. Access is via North or South Uist by causeway and bridge.	

FIRTH OF CLYDE

Arran	Brodick	**Ardrossan**
Arran	Lochranza	**Claonaig (1)**
Bute	Rothesay	**Wemyss Bay**
Bute	Rhubodach	**Colintraive**
Cumbrae	Cumbrae Slip	**Largs**
Dunoon		**Gourock**
Kilcreggan		**Gourock**

(1)   Seasonal service only between April and October.
(2)   Passenger only.
(3)   Carries vehicles between Easter and early October.
      Passengers only carried for the remainder of the year.
(4)   No caravans permitted on the island.

For more information contact:
      CALEDONIAN MACBRAYNE Ltd
      Head Office
      The Ferry Terminal
      Gourock
      PA19 1QP
      Tel. (0475) 33755 General Enquiries.

Bibliography

Munro's Tables and Other Hills of Lesser Heights (Scottish Mountaineering Club, 1990)

Gaelic-English Dictionary, McLennan (Acair & Aberdeen, 1989)

Heading for the Scottish Hills (Scottish Mountaineering Trust 1984)

Spur Book of Weather Lore, T. Brown and R. Hunter (Spur Publications, 1975)